BOULDER AMUSEMENT PARK

The Biography of a Carrousel

By Cyndy Hennig Hanks

Firefly Publications

2527 Baird Road
Penfield, New York 14526

ISBN: 0-9744541-0-9

Library of Congress Control Number: 2003095630

This project is made possible in part
with funds from the Decentralization Program, a regrant program
of the New York State Council on the Arts,
administered by the Genesee-Orleans Regional Arts Council.

State of the Arts

NYSCA

go Art!

Dedicated to
Lucille Morrot Walters and Paul Morrot
in honor of your father's legacy,
to the Indian Falls community,
and to my parents,
Marion Rose and Richard Leigh.

INTRODUCTION

More than 2,000 carousels were built between the late 1800s and 1930. The carousel was, and still is, recognized as the heart and soul of the amusement park. Amusement parks tended to be concentrated in large cities and the vacation resorts of the eastern seaboard. For most individuals, the only carousel they knew was the small traveling ride, which—if they were fortunate—came around once a year for one or two days before moving on. These are the carousels we typically associate with the Allan Herschell Company.

Less than 150 antique wooden carousels still operate, less than one-tenth of those that operated during the early 20th century. And yet, despite all the modern rides that overwhelm amusement park attendees today, the carousel is still the ride of choice for many children, as well as adults who have been captured by their charm and nostalgia. Many of today's enthusiasts are anxious to learn about carousels, particularly the carousels they rode in their youth. The more we learn and appreciate these rides, the more we become committed to their preservation.

Cyndy Hanks has been editor of the National Carousel Association's *Merry-Go-Roundup* magazine for more than 10 years, communicating her love for carousels and her dedication to their preservation. Ever since I first met and worked with Cyndy, she has been fascinated by the large, one-of-a-kind menagerie carousel that once operated at Boulder Park. This carousel has puzzled carousel experts for many years, and now the mystery has been solved.

Cyndy has woven her knowledge of carousels and her research into a book that helps us understand the lure of the carousel and of one carousel in particular. Reading this story, we realize that carousels are magical. What magic did we lose when this irreplaceable carousel was taken apart and sold piece by piece? We must do everything in our power to ensure that not even one more carousel is lost.

Brian Morgan
President, National Carousel Association
August 2003

FOREWORD

For more than 20 years, the community of Indian Falls, New York, wondered where the vanished carrousel went that whirled at Boulder Amusement Park. Some heard—and still believe—it went to Disneyland. Others heard it went to Texas and was consumed by a fire. Neither of these rumors is true.

In the 1980s, several unique, magnificently carved carousel figures were put up for auction. They created a stir. Collectors asked, what ride had the figures come from? When were they carved? One of the figures—a large white polar bear—was auctioned twice more, ultimately claiming the world's second highest price ever paid at auction for a carousel figure. Photographs of some of the figures appear in books and magazines, and some figures can be seen in museums and private collections, all with educated guesses about their origin. None of the guesses are accurate.

This is the true story of the one-of-a-kind carrousel designed by Emilie Morrot Bourgard—and of her brother, Theophilus John Morrot, who brought it to Boulder Park. In this book, the ride is called a carrousel, a merry-go-round, and occasionally a carousel: a carrousel, in deference to the name given it by the Allan Herschell Company, its manufacturer; a merry-go-round, in deference to what the ride was commonly called at the time; a carousel, when that more recent generic term fits.

It has taken more than ten years to research the biography of the carrousel I rode as a child. To do so, I traveled throughout the country, wrote scores of letters, consulted leading carousel experts, visited private carousel art collections and museums, researched the Morrot family genealogy, and now consider myself fortunate to call Lucille Morrot Walters and Paul Morrot friends.

A few months ago, when I was about to give up on ever finding information on one of Theophilus's brothers, Rose Babb called. Might she be related to the Morrots, through her mother, Rose, who was born in America 19 years after her grandfather emigrated? I learned Rose is Eugene Morrot's granddaughter, and some of her photographs appear in this book.

The book does have a happy ending: Lucille and Paul and Rose and her cousin, Worth Heath, reunited the family in June 2003.

CONTENTS

BOULDER AMUSEMENT PARK

A BOY AT SEA

*A*ugust 18, 1900. The passenger ship *Southwark* is steaming westward from Antwerp at 14 knots in the direction of New York Harbor, the big ocean waves smacking against the vessel's hull and heaving its cargo of immigrants up, down, and crabwise with a motion both relentless and unpredictable. This at first makes the boy queasy.

He looks about for distraction, his view largely obstructed by the squash of adults in steerage. His sister, Emilie, tells him there are nearly 900 passengers on this trip. He begins counting heads, but the task is too difficult. The squeamishness, however, passes.

Now a baby cries and then another, piercing the babble of foreign languages that surrounds him. Are we the only French, he wonders. As far as he can see, he is the only boy.

The passengers huddle in groups with their bundles, blankets, and pillows; all sorts of people he had never dreamed of, let alone experienced. He studies their expressions and observes their diversions.

Over there a group of men are playing cards. A girl, perhaps one of the men's daughters, helps an older woman who is seasick. To his left, a harmonica sounds plaintively.

Occasionally two or three people leave their group to venture a walk. The boy watches each weave their zigzag course through the steerage crush. Perhaps tomorrow he will persuade Emilie to climb with him to the deck, and perhaps they will get close enough to the rail to see the ocean.

Page 16: "The Steerage," by Alfred Stieglitz. Courtesy George Eastman House.

Below: "On Board Ship Bound for New York." Courtesy Brown Brothers.

The Morrot family in 1900. Front row, left to right: Theophilus J. Morrot (9), Jeannet and Eugenia Morrot (in France, Eugenia spelled her name "Eugenie"), and Morris Morrot (8). Back row, left to right: Jean-Pierre Morrot (22), Emilie Morrot Bourgard (24) and Pierre Bourgard (28), Ernest Morrot (29), and Henry Morrot (15). Eugene Morrot (20) is absent; he is with the French Cavalry. Courtesy the Morrot family.

It is now nine o' clock, he is nine years old, and the ship will be his home for the next nine days. *Neuf, neuf, neuf,* he thinks, and laughs at his own cleverness.

The boy is Theophilus John Morrot, the sixth child and fifth son of the hard-working and ofttimes intemperate Jeannet Morrot, a glassblower at the bottle factory in Reims, and his indomitable wife, Eugenia Faurobert Morrot. Emilie is the boy's only sister; yesterday she turned 25.

Emilie's formal appearance belies her predilection for flash, fun, and razzle-dazzle; she rides a bicycle. The boy, on the other hand, is more mature than his appearance indicates; he has already learned the importance of work and prayer and of being a self-made man. Despite the difference in age between sister and brother, the two connected early and are fast friends, preferring each other's company to that of their peers.

Theophilus pulls a folded piece of paper from his pocket and gives attention to a hand-written prayer, his lips moving silently.

Seigneur, je ne suis qu'un, voyageur sur la terre, je marche sur cette route paréc de vos richesses. Je les admire je vous en benis . . . mais ce n'est pas la mon veritable sé-jour je ne fais qu'i passer . . . .

[Lord, I am but one traveler on this earth . . . I travel this path because of your riches. I admire them, I have been blessed. But this is not my true stay. I am just passing through.]

More than a century later, Theophilus's daughter, Lucille, will pause at a photograph that has hung for years on the wall of her living room stairway, the steps leading to her bedroom. It shows Theophilus with his family in Reims a few days before the goodbyes. Lucille will wonder, which one is my father?

Theophilus looks at his daughter from the photograph, his eyes bright with the captured moment of excitement. He stands at the left in the front row beside his father. His mother is beside his father, and beside her, standing with his hoop, is Morris. Morris is the youngest, born in 1892.

In the back row, on the left, is Jean-Pierre, who goes by Pierre. He is the tallest, nearly six feet. He is married to Elise, and they live in Montreal. Next are Emilie and her husband, Pierre Bourgard, whose hand rests on her shoulder. Their first child, Kearie Jeanne, was born June 9 in Salem, New Jersey, and died July 19; a pity.

To Bourgard's right is Ernest. He's the one with the cigar. He is married to Clementine.

Which one is Henry?

Henry stands far right, behind Morris.

Which one is Eugene?

Eugene is not in the picture. He is away training with the French Cavalry.

Was Emilie the only girl?

Yes, and your father loved her dearly.

The Southwark *was a 8,607-gross-ton steamship built in 1893 by* Wm. Denny & Bros. *for the American Line. She was 480 feet long and 57.2 feet wide, with one funnel, four masts, and a twin screw.*

In 1895 she went to the Red Star Line and began her first Antwerp-New York run on August 31, 1895. By 1900, when the Bourgards and Theophilus sailed to America, the Southwark *could accommodate 250 second-class passengers and 929 third-class passengers. She made her last voyage from Antwerp to New York in 1903 and was then chartered to the Dominion Line. She was scrapped in 1911. Author's collection.*

On the second day of the journey, Theophilus stands at the rail and studies the ocean, waves now rising and falling with a strong regular rhythm. What is his mother doing now?

It is morning in Reims, and Eugenia is tending the chickens.

Poule, poule, poule, she calls as she scatters handfuls of corn over the ground.

Black hens, white hens, and a banty rooster suddenly encircle and entangle her feet; they live to eat. The older white chickens peck away furiously, crowding out their weaker companions—but they have been outsmarted. Eugenia deftly grabs one by its long, scrawny neck and lifts it straight up. A quick twist of the wrist, and the victim falls in a feathery heap. The others pause for a second; they are concerned only with eating.

A second white chicken, equally surprised, meets the same fate. Soon the two are beheaded and hanging upside down from the clothesline, awaiting the final indignity of the stewpot.

Tonight's dinner will feed only her, Jeannet, Henry, and Morris—the others have all gone. Next year she will take Morris to America, and the following year, Jeannet will take Henry.

On the fifth day of Theophilus's journey, his queasiness returns, but the cause is not seasickness. Instead, he has become all too aware of the pungent odor building up in steerage.

The next time he climbs to the deck and lingers, it is to take long, deep breaths of the fresh sea air.

Several days pass in similar fashion, and Theophilus makes more frequent visits to the upper deck.

One day while there, he meets Charles Binssel, a ten-year-old boy who also speaks French and travels with his father, mother, and younger sister and brother. They are going back home to America, to a town named Fairmont in the state of Indiana. Charles tells Theophilus he was born there. Despite their different dialects, the two carry on a conversation. Charles's father confirms Theophilus's suspicions; they are the only other French on the ship.

Today he has spent most of the day at the rail, watching for the first sign of land.

On the ninth day of his journey, he is again at the rail with Emilie when a jagged gray fringe appears at the horizon.

As the ship approaches, the fringe transforms itself into clumps of tall buildings.

Theophilus reports this observation to Emilie; she tells him the Americans call them "skyscrapers."

More rows of skyscrapers come into view and grow increasingly taller as the ship approaches. The panorama is magical, intimidating, and breathtaking. Such greatness surpasses everything he remembers of Reims, even the city's great cathedral. But unlike that city's greatness, America's greatness does not diminish him. It welcomes him, surrounds him, and enfolds him.

On their way into New York Harbor, they pass the Statue of Liberty.

The passengers on the deck crowd to that side, causing the ship to tilt. They remind Theophilus of chickens.

Emilie tells him the statue was a gift from the people of France to America; it is a symbol of their new freedom.

On August 28, the ship glides in. The passengers herd to the deck to await the harbor boat that will take them off and directly to the Barge Office, a turreted building of gray stone on the southeast tip of Manhattan, now taking the place of burned Ellis Island.

After they dock, the landed passengers are divided into groups that will, individual by individual, undergo immigration processing.

Theophilus asks, was Emilie frightened the first time she came to America?

"No, Pierre knew what to do."

"How did he know?"

"He had been to America before."

Bourgard's previous voyage to America—and Emilie's first—was in December 1898. They had married on August 13 that year, shortly before her 23rd birthday.

After the wedding, the couple told the family of their plans to live in America.

At last, America.

The new century has arrived, and already millions of immigrants have disembarked in America, believing they have exchanged the drudgery and political uncertainties of the past for an exciting future full of opportunity.

Here and abroad, the individual is gaining self-confidence, moving from an allegiance to God and His purpose for the individual to a competitive process in which the strongest and most aggressive are rewarded.

Socially, power is beginning to shift from the elite to the masses.

And technological advances in science and industry, such as electricity, the telephone, the automobile, and the airplane hold promise for even greater things to come. Courtesy Brown Brothers.

Theophilus replays the circumstances of her leaving, as he has done every day since then.

It was December 9, only three days before his eighth birthday and a fortnight before Christmas when she went out of his life.

Will she ever come back?

Will I see her again?

But more than a year later, a surprise. The couple came home for a visit. Emilie was flushed and excited. She and Bourgard extolled the virtues of living in America. There is much work and a bright future for craftsmen in New Jersey, they said, particularly in the glassmaking industry.

Theophilus, who had worked as a glassblowers' apprentice since the age of six, listened intently.

When the time came for the couple to return to America, he clutched his sister's hand and waved goodbye to his homeland.

"Horse and Wagon Days at Battery—Awaiting Immigrants." From 1890 to 1891, immigrants were processed at the Barge Office, a landing place in Battery Park on the southeast tip of Manhattan, while a new immigration station was being built on Ellis Island. The new station opened on January 1, 1892, and burned to the ground on June 14, 1897. From that date forward until December 16, 1900, immigrants were again processed at the Barge Office until the new building on Ellis Island opened on December 17, 1900. Courtesy Brown Brothers.

Now, exactly 10 days later, he takes his first steps on American soil, one of 8.8 million passengers who arrived here in the first decade of the new century.

"Keep moving, keep moving."

The immigrants are hustled and herded into the back of a building. Each is given a card bearing a letter and a number. The number is their identification on the ship's manifest, and the letter shows the aisle in which they are to stand while waiting.

"Keep moving, keep moving."

Eventually they stand before an unfriendly doctor with a piece of chalk. He examines their hands, rummages through their hair, and inspects their faces for signs of rash, poor color, or feebleness. He does not mark their foreheads. This is good, as anyone marked with an "x" is rejected.

Next they meet the stern eyes of a blue-coated immigrations inspector, who checks their names against the ship's manifest. He talks to Pierre.

"Names?"

Pierre responds, "Pierre Bourgard. Emilie Bourgard. And Theophilus."

"Who paid your passage?"

"Myself."

"How many dependents?"

"Brother-in-law."

"Have you ever been in prison?"

"No."

"Can you read and write?"

"Yes."

"Occupation?"

"Glazier."

"Is there a job waiting for you?"

"No." (This was a catch. Contract labor laws forbade immigrants from signing up for any work abroad.)

"Destination?"

"Salem, New Jersey."

The inspector writes, "Salem, N.Y."

"Where in Salem?"

"Ward Street."

For immigrants arriving between 1891 and 1954, immigration passenger lists provided information such as marital status, last residence, final destination in the United States, if ever in the United States before, when, where, and for how long, and if going to join a relative, the relative's name, address, and relationship. More questions were asked beginning in 1906 and 1907.

Above: "Intelligence Testing of Immigrants." Courtesy Brown Brothers.

Below: Passenger record. Courtesy The Statue of Liberty-Ellis Island Foundation, Inc.

Did you know glassmaking was the first industry in America?

When the Jamestown colony was established, the settlers brought with them a group of glassblowers, after the English Board of Trade decided glass production would be an ideal use for the limitless forests of the New World.

But the early glass factories were a failure, and throughout the 17th and early 18th centuries, the colonists were forced to import glass for their wine, windows, and tableware.

By 1880, glass was again being manufactured in America, more than 25 percent of it for common bottles.

Information courtesy of the Corning Museum of Glass.

Photograph from a glass plate negative, taken at an unidentified glass factory c.1900. Author's collection.

GLASS WORKS

*A*pril 30, 1905. Theophilus—now Theophile—14 years old and a full-time employee at Salem Glass Works on Fourth and Broadway in downtown Salem, New Jersey, has been summoned to replace the regular mold boy, after the boy was fired for refusing to spend another day near the furnace.

Outside, it is damp and chilly, a penetrating cold that has gripped the entire length of the south Jersey shore. On Broadway, even the giant oak shivers; it is now more than 300 years old, and its ancient branches cover more than a quarter acre of the nearby property.

Inside, Theophile perspires continuously as the oppressive heat assaults his eyes and his throat. He sits at the ready at the feet of the master blower or gaffer, holding open a hinged iron blow mold that has been placed on the floor to accommodate the gaffer's long pipe.

The esteemed gaffer, the "master of the chair," sits at an old wooden bench with wide, flat, iron arms; he is ready.

The gatherer is warming the iron blow-pipe—a hollow iron rod usually between four and five feet in length and weighing about 15 pounds—in the furnace, also called the "glory hole." The furnace maintains a constant temperature of about 2,500 degrees Fahrenheit; it takes at least 24 hours to melt the mixture of white Jersey sand, crushed limestone, and sodium carbonate into glass. The shop operates three such furnaces with 16 pots, a day tank with five rings, and a continuous tank with 19 rings.

"Glass Blower, Mold Boy, and Two Other Men Working in Glass-Making Plant, Grafton, W. Va.," by Lewis W. Hine (1908). Courtesy Library of Congress.

"Bill, a Carrying-in Boy, and Others in Canton Glass Works, Marion, Indiana (1908)," by Lewis W. Hine Courtesy Library of Congress.

The end product is a bottle, as the Salem Glassworks makes only hand-made flint, green, and amber glass bottles, of light and emerald green, amber, and blue. The bottles will hold beer, food, proprietary medicines, and perfumes.

The gatherer slowly twists the flared end of the gaffer's blowpipe in the molten glass in one of the pots, collecting a small gob, or gather. While constantly rotating the pipe to keep the hot glass from sagging or moving off center, he steps quickly to an iron table. He rolls the glowing gob back and forth on the table's iron surface to make it even on all sides.

He then transfers it to the gaffer, while rotating the blowpipe to prevent the gob from sagging.

Also continuing to rotate the blowpipe, the gaffer blows into it a calculated puff of air, just enough to expand the gob into a pear-shaped bubble. He then lowers the bubble into the mold.

"Boy."

Theophile closes the blow mold. The gaffer again blows through the pipe to expand the captive bubble, which now conforms to the exact shape of the mold.

"Boy."

Theophile opens the blow mold. The gaffer lifts the newly formed bottle out of the mold and inflates the patterned bottle to size.

"Boy."

An assistant approaches with a solid iron rod called a pontil, or punty iron, with a small gob of hot glass at the end. He touches the gob to the bottom of the bottle, adhering it to the punty iron, and then breaks the neck of the bottle off the blowpipe with a sharp rap.

"Boy."

The crack-off boy appears and removes the finished bottle from the punty iron in the same way. The telltale pontil mark will be polished away later.

None of this happens at a leisurely pace. The boys must anticipate when they will be needed and then move quickly, in a coordinated symmetry, before the molten glass "freezes." Any false move will provoke disaster. And so they hover, highly alert, to avoid wasting even a second.

Some days Theophile forgets he is in America. The glass-making process has changed little since the earliest times, and the tools are the same as those used in France. But he has an advantage over the American boys—in France, the boys start working at an earlier age. By the time he arrived in America, he had completed nearly four years of his apprenticeship—and now it has been nearly nine.

Neuf. He laughs.

At first Theophile's skills surprised the gaffer, who was put off by the boy's self-confident behavior and foreign mannerisms, and his fellow workers, who shared an unsympathetic attitude toward Catholics, snubbed him. But ultimately he earned their respect. He reported every day, worked as hard as any of the men, did not complain, and now was applying himself diligently in the company's night school.

Market Street in Salem, N.J. Author's collection.

Above: Pierre and Philomina.
Below: "Philomine Margeurite Bourgard, seven weeks and two days." ("Philomine" was how Emilie spelled Philomina.) Courtesy Rose Babb.

"*Down in southern New Jersey, they make glass. By day and by night, the fires burn on . . . and bid the sand let in the light. Big, black flumes shooting out smoke and sparks; bottles, bottles, of every tint and hue, from a brilliant crimson to the dull green that marks the death of sand and the birth of glass.*

"*From each fire, the white-heat radiates on the "blowers," the "gaffers," and the "carryin'-in boys." The latter are from nine to eighteen years of age, averaging about fourteen, and they outnumber the adult workers. A man with nothing, hailing from nowhere, can get an easy job at fair pay, if he has boys who are able to carry bottles. . . .*

"*The glass-blowers union is one of the most perfect organizations in the country. The daily wage runs from five dollars to twenty dollars, and from four to eight hours is a day's work. But the "carryin'-in" boys work nine and ten hours and get two dollars and a half and three dollars a week.*

"*Passing back and forth in the pale, weird light, these creatures are imps in both the modern and the old-time sense of the word. They are grimy, wiry, scarmy, scrawny, stunted specimens, and in cuss-words and salacious talk, they know all that grown men know. In the use of the ever surviving, if not ever fitting superlative, "damnedest," they are past masters all. Their education has consisted mainly of the thoughts, emotions, and experiences that resulted from contact with "blowers" and "gaffers," besides views of a big, barn-like space lit up by white-hot sand. This has been their universe at those times of day when they were most alive, most wide-awake, most sensitive to impressions.*

The manufacturers have endowed a night school, but (the teacher told me) the boys cannot keep their head up and their eyes open during the sessions, therefore their brains don't make much headway—God help them!

Yes, I think, God help them, for their eyes remind me of shriveled pansies, and I can't resurrect pansies, I can only see that the pansies have good soil to grow in, pure water, fresh air, sunshine, stars, and dew; and for companions they should have roses, carnations, asters, violets, sweet-peas,—and pansies that likewise are not shriveled."

Carl Sandburg, "Millville," from In Reckless Ecstasy *(1904).*

Above: "Boys Working on Night Shift in an Indianapolis Glass Works (1908)," by Lewis W. Hine. Courtesy Library of Congress.

Page 25: "Young Night Worker in Glass Factory (1908)," by Lewis W. Hine. Courtesy George Eastman House.

In fact, last week he had received an award of $3.00 and words of glowing praise from his instructor, Lizzie M. Clarke, for his honorable record.

"My dear Theophile," she wrote, "Your record this winter is especially pleasing for it is such a decided improvement upon your former behavior.

"I believe you have not a single thing against you in any way; your conduct has been absolutely blameless; your work excellent.

"It affords me much pleasure, therefore, to see you not only entitled to first prize, but to one of the beautiful medals as well.

"Be just as good a boy out of school as you are in, and there's no danger but that the man will be all right.

"Hoping we may have you with us next year, wishing you a happy life in the meantime, I remain—very sincerely your friend."

Her optimistic tone was in stark contrast to Pierre Bourgard's recent dire predictions. For, despite Pierre's earlier conviction that life in

America was immeasurably better than life in Reims, he was beginning to sound like his father-in-law.

"Automation is coming. Soon it will take away our jobs. Don't be caught idle."

Once, after hearing this, Theophile responded with impertinent questions: Was Uncle Pierre saying this merely to make him work harder?

Is "automation" simply a convenient excuse for Father to drink?

Or is it possible that Father and Uncle Pierre are afraid of a bogey?

"What I say is true, Theophile," Pierre said. "Automation has arrived in Europe, and it is coming here.

"Machines will replace us. It is only a matter of time." It was Uncle Pierre's frustration, and not his words, that ultimately convinced the boy the bogey was real.

Once he realized this, Theophile began seizing every opportunity to prove himself indispensable.

Already it appears to be working—Lizzie Clarke is on his side.

Theophile's brother Morris, now 12, appears. It is evening and time to leave. Morris works at the factory, as well. Eugenia had delivered him to Salem in July 1901 as planned, and, after a brief visit, returned to Reims.

Henry also appears; he and their father, Jeannet, came to Salem in February 1903. Both experienced glassmakers, they, too, found immediate employment.

The familiar drudgery of their day over, Jeannet and his sons walk into the night and give in to their fascination with the city and its glittering new arc and electric lights.

Soon Ernest, a molder, will leave Paris with his wife, Clementine, and go to New York City.

His mother—Theophile last saw her when she visited in 1904, when Emilie announced she was again pregnant.

On January 6, 1905, Philomina Marguerite Bourgard was born. She was to be the Bourgards' only child.

"Boy."

Theophile opens the blow mold.

"Boy."

Theophile shuts the blow mold.

"Boy."

Theophile opens the blow mold.

"Boy."

This command is for the carryin'-in boy, who rushes the finished bottle to the annealing oven for slow cooling.

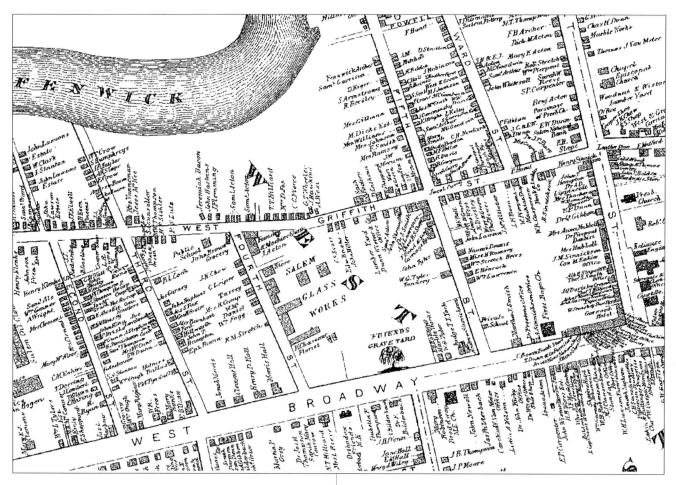

Top: Salem, New Jersey in 1875. When the Bourgards and Theophile first came to America, they stayed at 12 Ward Street with Pierre's stepfather, John Houvig. Pierre went by Peter Houvig in Salem, as he had already applied under that name for naturalization. In 1901, when he was naturalized as Peter Houvig, the Bourgards and Theophile lived on Miller Street. Author's collection.

Above: "The Old Oak, Salem, N.J. Height 88 Ft. Trunk 28' 2 in circumference, spreads 117 feet. Covers 1/4 of an acre, over 300 years old." Postcard postmarked 1908. Author's collection.

Occasionally the gaffer will hand Theophile the blowpipe, and with it the job of blowing. This is one of those days.

"Boy."

The gaffer signals Theophile to take his seat, as the gatherer collects another gob of molten glass at the end of the blowpipe.

The gaffer takes the blowpipe and passes it to Theophile. Turning the blowpipe continuously, Theophile blows a puff of air into the mouthpiece until a small bubble forms, then passes it back to the gaffer.

The gaffer takes over, further inflating the bubble.

Theophile resumes his previous position.

"Boy."

Theophile opens the blow mold.

"Boy."

Theophile closes the blow mold.

"Boy."

Theophile opens the blow mold.

This ritual continues, nine to ten hours a day, five days a week, and half-days on Saturday. At the end of the week, Theophile will receive $5.00 and count himself fortunate.

To Theophile and others at the factory, automation is still an imagined enemy. Glassblowing is a growing industry in America, the demand for glassblowers and their sons is at an all-time high, the white south Jersey sand is perfect and plentiful, and Salem Glassworks is a leading manufacturer in Salem County.

Nonetheless, the bogey is gaining ground.

By the end of the year, Michael Owens (backed by E. D. L. Libbey, owner of the Libbey Glass Company in Toledo) will have invented and perfected the automatic Owens Bottle Machine.

In 1906, the American Bottle Company in Streator, Illinois, will claim to be the first American bottle manufacturer to operate with fully automatic machines. The company's claim will include assurances, however, that its hand-blown operations will continue for several years.

By the time Theophile's brother, Eugene, and his wife and children arrive in Salem, in May 1906, new jobs for glassblowers will already be scarce.

In August 1907, Jean-Pierre and Elise and their stepdaughters, Lea and Louise Letellier, will leave Paris and go to New York City.

Theophile's mother, Eugenia, the last family member to leave Reims, will make Salem her home in 1907.

Top: Emilie and Pierre Bourgard with Philomina. Courtesy Rose Babb.

Above: Theophile (left) and Morris (right) Morrot. Courtesy Rose Babb.

Above: A carnival midway in the early 1900s, this one at Waterville, Maine. Such photographs are rare because so few carnivals were on the road then. Author's collection.

Left: A cartoon canine carnival. Author's collection.

EPIPHANY

*I*t is late summer 1907, or perhaps as late as 1909. The fatigued horse slows to a canter, granting the wagon and its road-weary occupants a respite from the harsh and constant jouncing, bouncing, and bumping of the last several hours.

Emilie and Theophile—now Theo— have made good time on this trip through Illinois, about six miles an hour over a dirt road that is little more than wheel tracks and ruts. Their journey so far has been uneventful, like the scenery with its long, flat stretches of woodland and farmland, interrupted only occasionally by clusters of roadside buildings.

The *Southwark* was kinder than this wagon, Theo comments, rubbing the back of his neck.

He studies the horizon, having spotted something unusual ahead.

"Whoa!"

A gasoline-powered automobile approaches in a huge cloud of dust, a rare and unnerving sight at the time, when such apparitions would easily frighten most horses. Theirs is no exception.

"Whoa. *Whoa!*"

They stop.

Theo steps down and walks slowly to the panicked horse, speaking quietly until it calms. He holds the bridle as the automobile passes. In a few moments they are once more on their way.

About an hour later, their progress again is interrupted.

"Whoa. Slow down."

The horse is skittish.

"Slow down."

Seeing nothing unusual, they listen.

Herschell-Spillman's new No. 1 Steam Riding Gallery, known as the Twenty-Four Horse machine. At one time, this company, having acquired the assets of the defunct Armitage-Herschell Company, was the largest manufacturer of merry-go-rounds in America. Courtesy Herschell Carrousel Factory Museum.

Up ahead, about a half mile and off the main highway, they discern the faint sounds of a midway, the sound of a great crowd, laughing and screaming.

The crowd gasps a collective "Oooooh." A pause, and then, "Aaaaah." More laughter. A cacophony of sounds and a tinkling mix of music, some of it organ chords, all of it festive.

As they approach, a warm evening breeze from that direction brings with it the alluring smells of food and now, more distinctly, the raucous ballyhoo of a carnival in full swing.

Soon a magical landscape unfolds before them—sparkling lights, a spinning Ferris wheel, glittering art, games of chance with racks of prizes, dancing girl shows, snake shows, and even freak shows.

A barker spots his easy marks—Theo and Emilie—and begins his spiel.

"Step right up. Step right up. What're you waiting for?

"She's *in there now*.

"She's *in there now*.

"Your *friends and neighbors* have seen her; come *in and see* what they're seeing.

"Your mind will *fail* to believe what your *eyes* will see.

"She's *in there now*.

"See the bearded lady.

"See the bearded lady inside. She's *inside*, folks, *inside*.

"Look through the doorway.

"She's *waiting* for you.

"She's *waiting* for you, and you're *just in time*."

The bearded lady and the other attractions were riveting enough, but the moment Theo would recall most vividly, the moment that would forever change the direction of their lives, was when he and Emilie stood, entranced, in front of the carnival's whirling merry-go-round.

The Bearded Lady. Many other "freaks of nature," such as Percilla, the monkey-girl, and Emmett, the alligator-skinned man, found not only jobs, but friendship and love while working for carnivals. The "freak shows" were of great interest to Theo. Author's collection.

BIRDSEYE VIEW OF HERSCHELL-SPILLMAN COMPANY'S PLANT
NORTH TONAWANDA, N. Y.

It was the custom of carnivals then to visit small towns for a week or two and then move on. By 1905, nearly 50 traveling shows were in existence, but by 1907, due to a money panic, this number was down to 33. However, C. W. Parker, "The Carnival King," put four shows on the road that year, employing 876 workers and filling more than 80 railroad cars with his attractions.

Other popular carnivals included Col. Francis Ferrari's wild animal show and Bostock's operation at the Jamestown Exposition, the Lackman-Loos Carnival Company show, the Johnny J. Jones Exposition Shows, and the Cole Younger (former outlaw) & Col. Nichols Amusement Company show.

The ice cream cone was a new attraction, following its introduction at the St. Louis Exposition. The Loop-the-Loop rides and high dives (into shallow tanks of water) were also highly popular on the larger midways.

In the rural areas, however, carnival attractions consisted mainly of rides, games, and concessions—generally a Ferris wheel, a merry-go-round, tests of skill, games of chance, sideshows, and food and drink. The merry-go-rounds were hand-carved, flying horses suspended from chains, made sturdy enough to withstand the wear and tear of travel, setup, and breakdown.

The ticket taker for the merry-go-round observes Theo and Emilie, who are still transfixed. When he finishes loading the children onto the flying horses, he walks over to them, twirls his thick black mustache, and confides, "Best little business in the world. I'm quitting tonight and going on the road tomorrow with my own merry-go-round. Then I'll be the boss."

Emilie asks him where carousels are made. A few days later, the Bourgards and Theo are aboard a train to the Herschell-Spillman Company factory in North Tonawanda, New York, where they put their earnings into a steam-powered, canvas-topped merry-go-round, a Number 1 Special.

Emilie and Theo's first merry-go-round. Courtesy the Morrot family.

Newspaper advertisement. Author's collection.

The company gave this description of its Steam Riding Gallery in its 1911 catalog:

"Our Improved Two-Horse Gallery is what is known as the Twenty-Four Horse machine. Listed as No. 1. It is 40 feet in diameter.

"This machine consists of 16 [wooden] sweeps fastened to the hub casting, which, in turn, is located on the center pole. These sweeps are supported by 16 cone-shaped track wheels, and they, in turn, run on the steel-faced circular track. These sweeps form the main framework of the machine.

"The inside and outside rockers are supported by the sweeps. These rockers are keyed to the same shaft, and derive their motion from the eccentric. Upon the platform of the machine are located 16 fine folding chairs, placed at the . . . edge of the platform, beside the horses and chariots. . . . The horses are located on the rockers."

The rocker arrangement produced a life-like galloping movement.

The horses, said the factory, were "carved by hand from well-seasoned poplar and by very expert mechanics." They had glass eyes and regular horsetails.

The chariots were also hand-carved, as well as upholstered, and "handsomely decorated."

The ride came with a Herschell-Spillman Company No. 37 military band organ measuring five feet high, with 44 keys and two barrels that played eight tunes each. The cabinet was made of white oak with a piano finish and gilded, engraved scroll-work.

Not only was the ride appealing, it was an ideal "carnie ride," designed for easy knockdown and setup.

Soon they were back on the road, but this time as their own enterprise. Theo did the setup work and maintenance, and Emilie—wearing black so the dust and grease from the machinery wouldn't show on her clothing—managed the business.

She rode the spinning carousel, stepping between the galloping herd, distributing tickets and making change from the bag slung over her shoulder.

Somewhere between 1907 and 1909, the Bourgards and the Morrots settled in Streator, Illinois, first appearing as residents in the city's 1909-1910 directory.

"They may have arrived sooner and lived here as boarders," suggests Rosemary Promenschenkel, assistant director for the Streatorland Historical Society, Inc.

The directory lists a "Peter Beauregard" (glassblower) and wife, "Emily," "John Morrit" and wife, "Eugenie," and Theophile and "Maurice Morrit" (both work at American Bottle Company) as residents at 121 West Hickory Street.

The following year, the city's 1911-12 directory lists a Peter "Beaurgard" (glassblower) and wife, Emily, and Theophile and Morris Morrot at 308 W. Morrell Street. Eugene and Amalia Morrot are listed as Eugene (works at American Bottle Co.) and "Emily", residing at 1111 North Park Street.

During the carnival season, Theo and the Bourgards traveled from carnival to carnival, returning to the American Bottle

Emilie and Theo on the merry-go-round wagon, which doubled as their home when they were on the road. The folding chair on the right was part of the ride. (See the Herschell-Spillman catalog illustration on page 29.) Courtesy the Morrot family.

Main Street, looking east, Streator, Illinois. Author's collection.

Right and below: Some time after 1912, Eugene and Amalia Morrot moved from Streator to an apple farm in Virginia. Courtesy Rose Babb (Eugene's granddaughter).

Company after the season.

Streator's location was ideal for glass production for several reasons: the abundance of Streator coal, an "inexhaustible supply of the best sand in the world," the city's central location, and an excellent railroad system.

By 1912, American Bottle was the largest producer of glass bottles in the world; the Streator works alone were turning out 740 bottles a minute.

In 1913, the company increased production to 5,000 gross of bottles per day, two million gross yearly. The factory employed 1,800 men, who were making mostly beer, water, and soft-drink bottles.

Despite the company's amazing success, Theo's daughter, Lucille, will not recollect him ever mentioning the American Bottle Company, only "all the carnivals they worked while they lived in Streator."

For several years, the Bourgard family and Theo traveled throughout the United States and Canada, moving from carnival to carnival, their living quarters a glorified, horse-drawn hay wagon with sides and a roof. At night, Theo pulled canvas around the merry-go-round and slept on the floor or left his two fox terriers, Sport and Rosy, on guard.

When their merry-go-round ultimately wore out, Emilie and Theo returned to North Tonawanda for a replacement and continued their operation.

At some point, they ended up in Missouri, where they operated a movie theater during the off season.

Emilie and Theo's second merry-go-round. Courtesy the Morrot family.

Frank James, the legendary outlaw and brother of equal legend Jesse James, sold tickets for them; years later Theo will tell his children about the time when Frank James worked for them at the theater in Missouri and what a pleasant and polite man he was. Theo also told his children he traveled with Blue Ribbon Shows out of Tennessee and Kentucky.

Motion pictures became popular attractions at the carnivals, after successful showings of *The Great Train Robbery* during the 1905 season. The showmen purchased special black "motion picture tents" for this purpose, which proved a wise investment. Now people were lining up early in the morning outside the tents, and many of them returned again and again to see the same show.

This new form of amusement was at first incredibly profitable for the carnival showmen, but eventually it would steal their customers.

Last picture of legendary outlaw Frank James, taken at his farm near Excelsior Springs, Missouri. Author's collection.

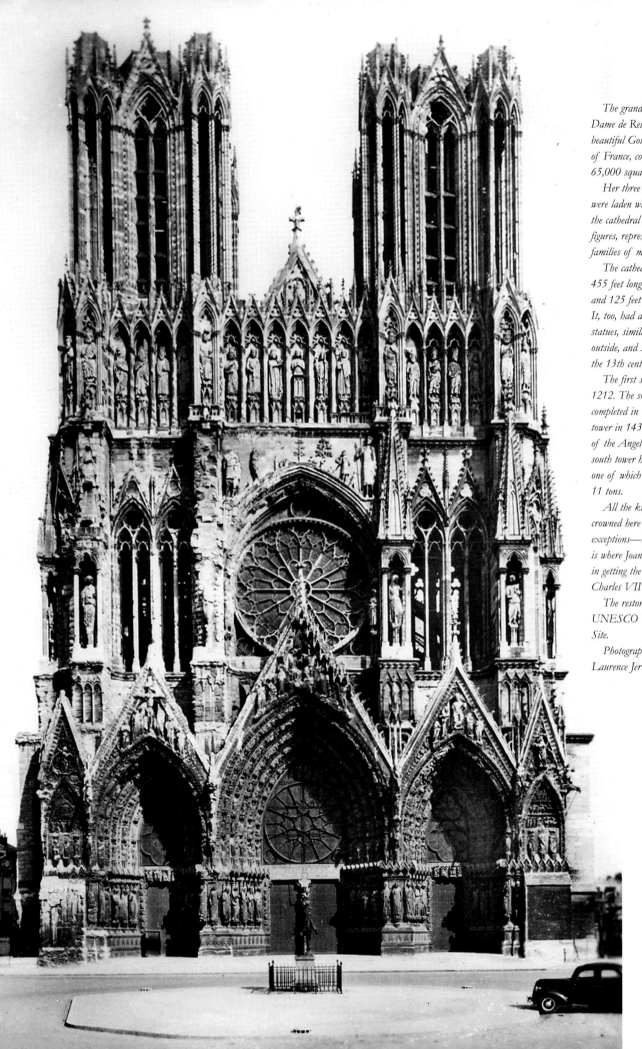

The grand Cathedral Notre Dame de Reims, the most beautiful Gothic structure in all of France, covered approximately 65,000 square feet.

Her three exterior portals were laden with statuary. In all, the cathedral had nearly 5,000 figures, representing nearly all the families of mankind.

The cathedral's interior was 455 feet long, 98 feet wide, and 125 feet high in the center. It, too, had a profusion of statues, similar to those on the outside, and stained glass from the 13th century.

The first stone was laid in 1212. The south tower was completed in 1391, the southwest tower in 1430, and the Belfry of the Angel in 1497. The south tower held two great bells, one of which weighed more than 11 tons.

All the kings of France were crowned here with only four exceptions—26 in all. And this is where Joan of Arc triumphed in getting the dauphin crowned as Charles VII in 1429.

The restored cathedral is a UNESCO World Heritage Site.

Photograph from France, by Laurence Jerrold, 1916.

REIMS

June 28, 1914. The carnival season is at peak, and towns and villages all over America are making plans for the Fourth of July. Decatur, Illinois, for example, plans a balloon ascension, pie- and bun-eating contest, and a "Jesse James Wild West Show."

The moving-picture theaters will be filled to capacity; their popularity is increasing by leaps and bounds. In some areas, the demand for "Westerns" is such a craze that it has created a labor problem for the cattlemen— too many cowboys are trying to get in the movies. The Bourgards and Theo, if they should hear this about carnivals and movie theaters, must be convinced they are in the right place at the right time.

The day also started beautifully in the small city of Sarajevo, the capital of Austria-Hungary's restless province of Slavic Bosnia, and the city was astir with anticipation. Elegantly dressed men and women crowded Sarajevo streets, for it was Serbian fete day, and the Archduke Francis Ferdinand and his consort, the Duchess of Hohenberg, would be motoring through in their royal car, en route to a military inspection.

But dark forces were at work to prevent the occasion from happening. Shortly after noon and a brief episode of violence, a political zealot assassinated the Archbishop and the Duchess.

The next day, the American press assures its readers that the assassination was just another "mess in the Balkans." To the majority of Americans, who are accustomed to peace, the news is merely a temporary intrusion from a distant and alien world. They pause for a second, then life goes on.

The people of Reims, on the other hand, interpret the event with great uneasiness.

One of the cool, dry chalk caverns under the city of Reims. These were once chalk quarries, but later became the even-temperatured cellars so vital to the maturing of the delicate wine. During World War I, when Reims was under bombardment, these cellars became an underground city with churches, courts, schools, and living accommodations for 20,000 people. Author's collection.

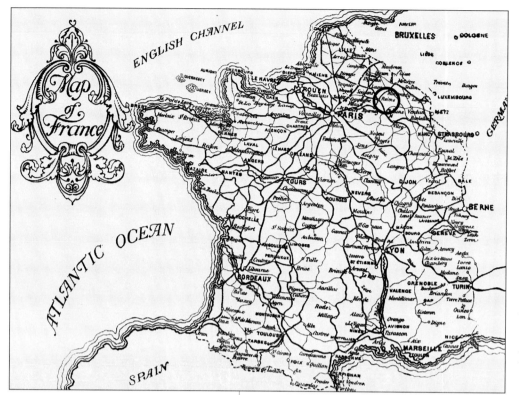

Reims, the shrine of France, in the province of Champagne, sits on a broad plain on the right bank of the river Vesle, and on a canal that connects the Aisne with the Marne. To the city's south and west are the "montagne de Reims" and rolling, vineyard-clad hills, and even further southwest is Paris.

The city enjoys a rich history and magnificent Gothic structures: The Cathedral de Notre Dame (completed before Columbus discovered America), the triumphal Roman arch, the Porte de Mars (Reims' oldest structure), the 11th-century Abbaye/Basilica St.-Remi, the Palais de Tau, and various museums of archeology, art, and local history. Delicate, sparkling white wines from the province of Champagne mature in the cool, dry chalk caverns under the city; champagne is made only from the

Top: Map of France, from The Cathedrals of Northern France, *by Francis Miltoun, illustrated by Blanche McManus, 1903. The Morrot family was living in Reims then.*

Above and page 39: Reims before and after the bombardment by the Germans. Author's collection.

grapes grown around Reims and nearby Epernay.

Reims has an independent spirit, and a dialect and French accent all its own. And in Reims, as in all of France, the "cult of the individual" reigns supreme—what is best for individuals and their families comes first, before any allegiance or governance.

Before the assassination in Sarajevo, Reims shared Europe's hopes and plans for international peace.

It had been more than 40 years since France's last war, all the unclaimed territories on other continents had been claimed, and Europe had advanced all the backward regions of the world. It was entirely possible, her people believed, that the world had finally outgrown war.

Until the assassination.

Despite the initiatives toward world peace, international tension was high. In Austria, the sentiment was growing daily that the world's nations were moving toward a major conflict. French nationalists argued that Germany's threat to French security must be met by increased preparedness. "Russia is ready. France must be ready too," they urged.

"The whole of Germany is charged with electricity," said Colonel House, chief advisor to President Woodrow Wilson, who was dispatched to Berlin in May. "It only needs a spark to set the whole thing off."

To further complicate matters, the nations of Europe were living in a state of anarchy. Each of them—sovereign states all—refused to recognize any authority higher than its own and each refused to accept any idea that diminished its ability to create its own allies, declare its own wars, strike its own bargains, or do anything it pleased, even at the cost of war.

Until the assassination.

France had already lost its iron deposits and mines, its iron and steel

363   REIMS. — La Place du Marché. — Market Place.

18764   Ruins of Once Magnificent Reims, France

"Before us lies Reims (remz), torn, smashed, blown to fragments, but unconquerable. For two years a storm of shot and shell rained upon the devoted city. High explosives blew out roofs, caved in walls, dug caverns in the streets, but still the city held out. Before the war 120,000 people lived here; after the war but 2,000 could find a place to lay their heads. Like so many other French cities and villages, Reims is a monument to German vandalism. The enemy could not capture it, so they smashed it. In 1914, when the Germans held the city for eleven days and expected to make it their headquarters, no damage was done. Driven out, they turned their fury upon it, sparing not even the glorious cathedral. No tongue can describe the destruction that was wrought. The section of the city that is before us is bad enough—bare walls, rooms gaping open to the sky, twisted iron stanchions and piles of debris. But there are a few houses standing, here and there, a few roofs left. In other sections, for block after block, there is not a roof, not a fragment of wall ten feet high. Piles of crumbled stone half the height of a man litter the sidewalks for thousands of yards—for in Reims there were no frame houses, all were of stone. These piles of debris, these jagged walls, these chambers open to the sky are covered in a pall of white dust— plaster blown into powder—a scene of utter desolation. One who has not seen cannot believe such destruction possible. But we have it before us. We see the empty rooms, the tottering walls, and the charred and broken fragments. This is what the war has left of Reims, one of the finest cities of France." Stereoscope and caption from the author's collection.

plants, and its large textile mills to Germany with the cession of Alsace-Lorraine, and the country was still paying down a war indemnity of $5 billion francs. Even so, France would not have declared war on Germany, nor would she have subjected Europe to the horrors of war, even to win back Alsace-Lorraine.

On August 4, Germany invaded Belgium, though bound by treaty to respect that country's neutrality. This utter disregard of the neutrality rights of an innocent and peaceful nation was a travesty beyond the world's belief.

Germany's plan knew no mercy; its goal was to crush France before Russia could mobilize, then turn eastward to crush the forces of the Czar.

By August 24, Austria-Hungary had declared war on Russia and Belgium, France and Great Britain had declared war on Austria, Serbia had declared war on Germany, and Montenegro had joined Serbia against Austria and Germany.

With the German advance underway, an attack on Paris, and perhaps even Reims, was inevitable. The Battle of the Marne began September 5, but it did not go well for Germany. The determined French annihilated one German army in short order and sent the other two into retreat. Paris was saved. The Allied armies were intact.

The enraged Germans spent their fury on Reims.

They fired on the grand cathedral, claiming its towers were needed for observation purposes. But that was not true—the undefended cathedral was devastated in a deliberate act of vengeance. The damage was pure vandalism, an act of ruthless and reckless barbarism. When the Germans were finished, the once-magnificent city of Reims was laid flat.

Now as the 1914 carnival season concludes, Theo is 24 and unmarried. Eugene and Jean-Pierre are with the French cavalry, fighting the war. Ernest, Henry, and Morris have enlisted in the U.S. Army. Jeannet, their father, has become increasingly unreliable and cannot be trusted to care for their mother, Eugenia. Reims is devastated; all that remains are memories.

Will Theo accept responsibility for Eugenia?

He does.

As time passes and the war continues, postcards and letters arrive from the battlefronts, occasionally with enclosed photographs, bearing assurances that his brothers are fine.

In 1917, America joins the conflagration—at the perfect moment, as far as the French are concerned. This news raises the soldiers' morale and revives the French government's hopes that in time victory is possible.

In their father's footsteps: Jeannet Morrot, the father of Ernest, Jean-Pierre, Henry, Theophilus, and Morris, in 1890, the year Theophilus was born. Courtesy Rose Babb.

When the Armistice is signed on November 11, 1918, World War I—the bloodiest war in human history, ended in victory, but at the cost of nearly 8,500,000 lives and 30 million more injured.

Henry is injured but survives, and Ernest and Jean-Pierre are among the dead. One of them, either Ernest or Jean-Pierre, was killed by the Germans when he was on his way home, after the Armistice was signed.

Left: Jean-Pierre Morrot sent this photograph to his family, with a note on the back, "I have just fed these chickens." Photograph courtesy Rose Babb.

Above, left: Henry owned a successful bar in Paris.

Above, right: Henry in uniform.

Below, left and right: Morris in uniform. Photographs courtesy of the Morrot family.

Top, right: Ernest Morrot (left) died in World War I as a U.S. Army soldier. The soldier on the right is unidentified. Courtesy the Morrot family.

Top, left and above: Jean-Pierre Morrot (marked "×" in group photograph). Courtesy Rose Babb.

Above: Jean-Pierre Morrot was a soldier in the French cavalry (marked "×" in photograph). He died in World War I. Photograph courtesy Rose Babb.

EMILIE'S CARROUSEL

Autumn 1919. John Wendler, a partner at the struggling Allan Herschell Company, sits back in his worn oak desk chair and regards with some interest the couple seated before him. Theirs is an ambitious proposal at the worst possible time.

The woman is mannerly and well dressed. Her long dark hair is arranged in a tidy French roll, from which only a few wisps have strayed. She appears older than her companion, but not enough to be his mother. The young man introduces her as his sister; there is a strong resemblance. She has a bright, open expression and determined smile.

The young man appears self-confident and at ease. His thin, dark hair recedes at the temples, and his favorite cap, now resting on his lap, has irreversibly crimped it. His hands are those of a laborer, and he speaks with the assurance of one who has found his calling.

Their second merry-go-round has worn out, they tell Wendler. They need a replacement, and they would like one built and delivered to Olcott Beach, New York, in the spring of 1920, before the next season begins. But this time, they do not want a standard catalog merry-go-round. No, Emilie has designed their third merry-go-round herself, and they would like it built to her specifications.

Emilie speaks with a delightful French accent. She has a musical voice, filled with enthusiasm. Her merry-go-round, she tells Wendler, will dazzle its beholders. It will have not only beautiful horses and elegant chariots, she says, but also seven large and realistically carved menagerie figures: a tall giraffe, a

Page 44: The Allan Herschell Company carving shop in 1919.

Above: Typical Herschell steeds, carved in the Country Fair style. Photographs courtesy Herschell Carrousel Factory Museum.

Top: The Allan Herschell Company factory building in 1919.

Above: Allan Herschell, president of the Allan Herschell Company in 1919. Photographs courtesy Herschell Carrousel Factory Museum.

Page 47: The Landow-Newman carousel. One of the horses from this primitive ride is at the Circus Hall of Fame in Sarasota, Florida. From A Pictorial History of the Carousel, *by Frederick Fried.*

two-hump camel, a deer with real antlers, a stalking lion and fierce tiger; in addition—(she leans toward him, pausing for dramatic effect)—hers will be the first merry-go-round in the country with an elephant and a white polar bear.

Her small hands flutter as she describes her creation, and he is charmed. Her creation will have 1,200 electric lights and a double row of mirrors in the center to reflect the lights. Between the mirrors will be original oil paintings. It will be an unforgettable merry-go-round. People will come from far away to ride it. And once they have ridden it, they will never forget it.

He hates to disappoint them, but he does it. Business is not what it was before the war. Only a few merry-go-rounds were produced then, and even fewer merry-go-round companies are back in operation. The shortage of materials is still critical, and the industry lost workers to the war. It may take an entire generation to replace those who died or were so badly injured that they are no longer fit for employment.

"If you must have the merry-go-round by spring," he says, "perhaps you should go elsewhere."

But they will not hear of it.

They are prepared to pay what the factory requires, the young man—Theo—says, to complete the merry-go-round by spring.

Wendler, who is known as a forward-thinking businessman, agrees to look at Emilie's drawings, and so she spreads them out.

To his surprise, they are quite good. She has designed a 35-foot park machine with 32 jumping horses, three abreast. The seven menagerie animals are spectacular, but within the capabilities of the

factory carvers. The outer-row horses are elaborately carved and have decorative trappings and jewels; the smaller inner-row steeds are standard and easily produced. The machine's incongruence makes it all the more appealing.

Wendler has never seen such a carousel, nor has the factory produced one—it would make an incredible showpiece.

Wendler has taken a liking to Theo and Emilie and decides to accept their order. Before he reveals his decision, however, he asks how they came to be in the merry-go-round business. As they reply, he muses at their passion and determination. It mirrors his own.

Then he shares his own story.

In 1879, at the age of 10, he watched Carl Landow build a carousel, one of the first of its kind in America. Landow was a German immigrant and cabinetmaker who lived in Wolcottsburg (now Clarence Center, New York).

He took issue with his community's sentiment that amusements were works of the devil, and in an act of defiance, carved crude horses from basswood, painted them bright colors, gave them real hair tails, and persuaded his unwilling brother-in-law, Carl Newman, to build a platform and turning mechanism for them.

Landow then set up his evil device on the grounds of a local tavern and invited the God-fearing community to ride it for a nickel. Wendler chuckles as he recalls a headline that appeared in the local newspaper the next day: "Merry-go-round: Carousel is a devil's device, bound to bring ruination to your children."

Despite the protests and Newman's pessimism, however, the community received the ride enthusiastically—so enthusiastically that Landow took it on the road to other locations and later replaced his human turners with steam power. When eventually Landow and his human band organ drank themselves into debt, Wendler's uncle ended up with the machine, in lieu of a loan payment.

Wendler walks Emilie and Theo toward the carpenter shop.

He tells them he came to the factory in 1889, when it was owned by the Armitage Herschell Company, to work as a horse painter. Within a short time, he was promoted to foreman, and the company became highly successful.

The company was depositing so much money at the banks that the banks finally refused to take its deposits—so the company invested heavily in land. In 1899, the real estate market collapsed, taking Armitage Herschell with it.

The standard "New Model Horses" produced by the Allan Herschell Company were designed for easy travel. Their heads were large, their ears folded back, and their legs tucked under their compact bodies. The cropped-mane-style horse (right) became quite popular. Courtesy Herschell Carrousel Factory Museum.

New Model Horses

ALLAN HERSCHELL CO., INC.

Allan Herschell and his brother-in-law, Ed Spillman, acquired the defunct company's assets, forming the Herschell-Spillman Company, with Wendler as foreman and superintendent. Herschell-Spillman became even more successful than its predecessor, producing more carousels than any other company in the world.

Herschell was plagued with ill health, which forced his retirement. He sold his interest in Herschell-Spillman, agreeing not to build any more carousels and to work only as a consultant. But before long, he cancelled this agreement and returned to the carousel business, forming the rival Allan Herschell Company in 1915. Wendler and Fred Fritchie went with him as partners.

The Herschell-Spillman company still operates, Wendler tells them as they reach the carving room, but much of its machinery was converted for war production.

Once inside, he tells them. The Allan Herschell Company will build Emilie's merry-go-round, and its figures will be hand carved by these experienced men, many of them German immigrants.

It takes Theo and Emilie a few seconds to absorb this revelation. He pauses.

"Shall we continue?"

He sees by their expressions that he has triggered some sadness, then recalls their account of Reims's devastation.

"Continue," Theo replies.

"This is Herman Jagow. He started out hand-carving horses for Herschell-Spillman in 1901, and joined the Allan Herschell Company in 1915. Now he focuses on heads, necks, and tails." (Jagow will continue carving until the day he retires, on June 12,

1946. He will die the day after, at the age of 70.)

"Meet Harry Nightengale . . . Fred Roth . . . Charles Blouier. They also carve heads, necks, and tails. 'Farmer Bill' Jagow; he carves bodies.

"Pete Flach also carves bodies [he will carve some 18,000 horses entirely by hand before he retires].

"And Jake Wurl. Jake's brother, Charlie, worked for me at Herschell-Spillman as a painter. When Allan Herschell left the company in 1913, Charlie went with him to the old greenhouse factory, which is now this factory. Herschell spent two years cleaning it up and building the roundhouse. The Allan Herschell Company started making carrousels in 1915."

Charlie persuaded Jake—a jack-of-all-trades in the paint shop at Herschell-Spillman—to join them.

"The roundhouse was brand new when I got there," Wurl said. "I worked in the paint shop until Labor Day, when Wendler here brought me over to Ward Oliver, who was foreman of the woodcarving shop. 'I want you to make a woodcarver out of him,' he said. That was a relief. I was actually afraid of those guys in the paint shop because of their horrible language and lack of respect for each other.

"I began carving the next day. I started with legs and made legs, legs, legs. They called me the leg man. Three or four guys were making legs and as many were carving heads. I learned by watching and trying."

"Wally [Ward] Oliver is foreman of the woodcarving and paint departments. He designs the horses and animals and supervises their construction. He painted scenery panels back when the factory was doing that. He learned from his father, who worked as an artist for Armitage Herschell.

"Joe Bronson—he just came in—just joined the factory. He's a horse painter. And this is Jack Fuller, who has had several different jobs here since 1915."

Most of what went on during the construction of Emilie's carrousel is lost to history, except for the elephant crisis:

The white polar bear, the most renowned menagerie figure on Emilie's carrousel. It was carved in either 1919 or 1920, before spring 1920. It has a red harness with tassels and decorative jewels. Allan Herschell Company factory photograph (1920). Courtesy the Morrot family.

Emilie's carrousel (1920). This elephant rode the platform only briefly, as it was too heavy and had to be removed. It was replaced with a smaller elephant. Allan Herschell Company factory photograph. Courtesy the Morrot family.

A Wurlitzer model 153 military band organ. The same model was on Emilie's carrousel. Author's collection.

Emilie's corpulent beast was simply too large and heavy for the ride. This fact wasn't discovered until construction of the ride was completed and the magnificent beast was placed on the platform. Despite the elephant's elegant appearance, it threw the machine off balance and had to be removed. It was replaced by a smaller, less elaborate creation about the same weight as the polar bear, which was then placed on the opposite side to keep the ride in balance.

The banished elephant resided in a corner of Allan Herschell's private office for a time, where Herschell kept banging into it. One day, after a particularly nasty bang, he hollered, "Get that damn thing out of here!"

The elephant disappeared soon after.

Of the carrousel's large outside-row horses, the lead horse was the most elaborate. It was a plumed, armored horse bearing a shield with a Crusader's cross.

Several of the completed figures were taken to a wood

carvers' exhibition in Chicago, where they won prizes.

Emilie's dream machine was delivered to Olcott Beach in the spring of 1920, and is now known as one of the only six or seven carousels built by the Allan Herschell factory between 1917 and 1920.

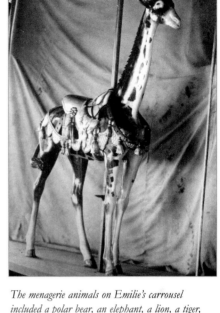

The menagerie animals on Emilie's carrousel included a polar bear, an elephant, a lion, a tiger, a giraffe, a two-hump camel, and a deer with real antlers. All were deeply carved and decorated with tassels and glass jewels. Photographs courtesy the Morrot family.

Olcott Beach, on the south shore of Lake Ontario, was a popular summer resort. Its sublime setting held an irresistible attraction for residents of the nearby city of Lockport, who traveled there regularly to picnic amid Olcott Beach's majestic pine trees in the Pine Tree Grove, splash in its sparkling blue water, and watch its fiery sunsets.

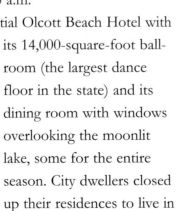

In summer, an electric trolley brought picnickers to Olcott Beach from various stops in western New York, with two or three loads arriving every half hour starting at 5 a.m.

Many lingerers stayed at the palatial Olcott Beach Hotel with

its 14,000-square-foot ball-room (the largest dance floor in the state) and its dining room with windows overlooking the moonlit lake, some for the entire season. City dwellers closed up their residences to live in the summer cottages along the resort's lakefront bluff.

The old merry-go-round in the park at Olcott Beach. This picture was taken in the early 1900s. Courtesy Frederick Fried Archives.

Olcott Beach enjoyed a succession of popular merry-go-rounds. The first, an Armitage Herschell Company Electric Riding Gallery, was installed before the turn of the century. The ride was so popular that it was replaced with a "new and improved one" in 1903.

By 1904, steamboats were making round trips to and from the cities of Rochester, LeRoy, Batavia, and Toronto. Olcott Beach's Main Street turned into a midway. A miniature railroad carried regular runs of visitors through the majestic pine grove, and the Rustic Theater offered vaudeville acts six days a week (the shows were free to those who arrived by trolley).

The International Traction Company opened Rialto Amusement Park at Olcott Beach in 1912 on land purchased across the street from the pine grove, adding a baseball diamond, another merry-go-round, and various amusement devices, such as a figure-eight roller coaster. It also offered concessions and games, a photography stand, and a fortune teller.

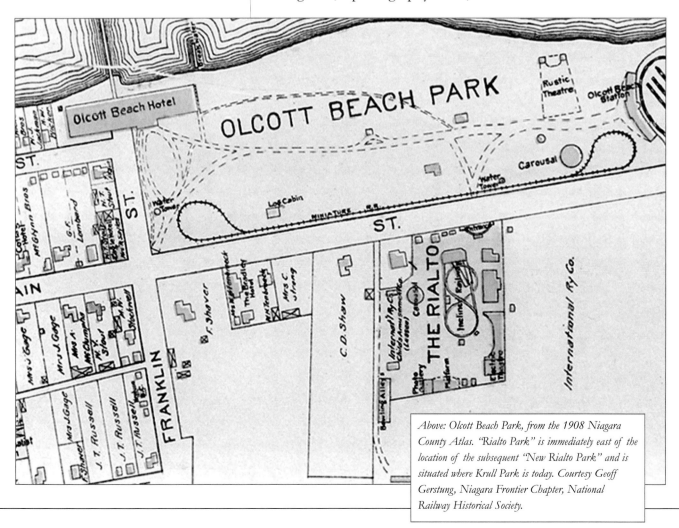

Above: Olcott Beach Park, from the 1908 Niagara County Atlas. "Rialto Park" is immediately east of the location of the subsequent "New Rialto Park" and is situated where Krull Park is today. Courtesy Geoff Gerstung, Niagara Frontier Chapter, National Railway Historical Society.

Left: The Arundel docks at Olcott Beach (1900-1920). The steamer ran from Charlotte to Oswego and the Thousand Islands in New York State. Courtesy Rochester Public Library.

Olcott Beach was the most popular lake resort in western New York until 1917. Theo and Emilie operated their second merry-go-round there at a profit, and Emilie began sketching her dream merry-go-round.

But a new bogey had its own destructive plan.

America's entry into World War I that year had a devastating effect on the country, the Olcott Beach business community, and Theo and Emilie's operation in Rialto Park. Attendance and profits declined as the lines of customers waiting to ride the merry-go-round became shorter and shorter.

Ultimately, after satisfying its bloodthirst and taking Ernest and Jean-Pierre, the bogey departs. Emilie and Theo remain undaunted.

Now, in 1919, Emilie has completed her drawings, she and Theo have delivered them to the Allan Herschell Company, and John Wendler has agreed to build the ride before spring.

The time has arrived, Wendler has just informed them. Emilie's carrousel is ready for testing.

When Theo and Emilie arrive at the factory, Emilie's carrousel is already circling slowly in the roundhouse. But there is little room to walk around it, as the factory had previously been producing the smaller, portable rides.

"As darkness falls and the crowd begins to thin out, the first notes of the band announce the dancing has begun. Early homebound revelers, making their way to the station, listen as the sweet strains of the new "Merry Widow Waltz" come floating through the grove and softly die away among the pine trees. When the band plays "Home, Sweet Home," it is time to start for home. Everyone is in a hurry to reach the station, where long lines of cars are waiting to transport the happy throng from Dreamland back to the realities of a workaday world." From Lockport Legends (1953), publication unknown. Courtesy Niagara County Historical Society.

Above: The entrance to Rialto Park at Olcott Beach, where Theo, Emilie, and Pierre first operated Emilie's carrousel and other amusement rides. Courtesy Geoff Gerstung, Niagara Frontier Chapter, National Railway Historical Society.

Above: A postcard showing the popular miniature railroad at Olcott Beach. Theo, Philomina, and Emilie are seated on the popular train ride. Author's collection.

Right: Emilie, Philomina, and Theo on the train.

Page 55: Theo and Emilie with their popular Ferris wheel, which also turned at Olcott Beach. Photographs courtesy of the Morrot family.

Wendler gradually increases the carrousel's speed, to an exhilarating seven revolutions per minute, which it is designed to operate at (the rides then whirled much faster than those of today). The carrousel turns smoothly.

He increases the speed again, and now the carrousel is spinning, pulling with it the room air. Theo, standing at the wall, finds it increasingly difficult to breathe and begins to feel faint. Just in time, Wendler shuts down the ride.

"Damned good machine," he declares.

When Theo and Emilie open Rialto Park for the 1920 season, Emilie's carrousel is the main attraction. People wait in long lines to ride it, and, having ridden, return again and again to ride it once more. News of the carrousel spreads, and soon Rialto Park fills with enchanted customers.

At the start of the season, the family lives on Allen Street in Lockport; the 1920 city directory lists "Eugenie" Morrot, Peter Bourgard (Lockport Glass Co.), Theophilus Morrot ("laborer, machine shop" and "operating carousel at Olcott"), "Emily" and "Philomina" Bourgard, Morris Morrot ("die cutter, HR Radiator Works") and his young wife, Eleanor ("born in Canada, from Minnesota"), as residents. (This is the only year Morris and Eleanor are listed.)

By the end of the season, Emilie's carrousel has generated enough income to enable the Morrots and the Bourgards to move to a stately two-story brick house on Gooding Street, near Monroe.

The house sits up high on a hill, surrounded by tall trees and far back from the

street, its spacious lawn edged with a wrought-iron fence. It reminds Theo of the homes in old France, with their cupolas, dormers, arches, and gimcrackery. All it needs is chickens.

On November 9, 1920—a few weeks before his 30th birthday—Theo becomes a naturalized United States citizen. He has now realized his American dream.

The popularity of Emilie's carrousel continues to increase, as does America's enthusiasm for the whirligigs. In later years, Jake Wurl, the woodcarver at the Allan Herschell Company, will recall, "1920 to 1928 were booming years for merry-go-rounds. We worked 10 hours a day from February through July Fourth.

Above: The house on Gooding Street in Lockport, where Theo and Eugenia Morrot and the Bourgard family lived during the early 1920s.

Left: Peter Bourgard, Eugenia Morrot (seated), and Peter and Emilie's daughter, Philomina. Photographs courtesy the Morrot family.

Left: Emilie and Theo. Theo's cap is similar to the Gatsby cap that became popular in America after 1925—and was as ubiquitous then as the baseball cap is today. He wore this style long before 1925, however. Courtesy the Morrot family.

"Some days we'd work 10 or 12 hours, eat supper, and then go back again."

As the Allan Herschell Company continues to prosper, John Wendler assumes additional responsibility as vice president and general manager. He will become the company's president in 1945.

"Every spring, tramps would come down the railroad tracks with their carving tools in their pockets. They'd go to Wendler and ask for work. They'd strike a deal, and nobody knew how much they got," Wurl continues.

"Them guys, they were artists. They had more skill than many people who were well educated. One guy had Parkinson's disease—he carved faces on shields, and for him it was second nature.

"As they came, that's the way they went."

Above: Morris and Eleanor Morrot. Courtesy the Morrot family.

Left: Jeannett Morrot, husband of Eugenia and father of Ernest, Emilie, Jean-Pierre, Eugene, Henry, Theophilus, and Morris Morrot, was born in France on March 12, 1851. Theo's son, Paul, has a paper on which Theo wrote his father's name with the comment,"Came to our home May 23, 1916." The 1917-1918 Lockport, New York city directory lists Eugenia Morrot as "widow of John." The 1920 federal census, however, lists John as an inmate at St. Sophia's Home/Little Sisters of the Poor, in Richmond, Virginia, which is confirmed by family records. Jeannet died in Virginia on November 24, 1922 and is buried in Richmond. Courtesy Rose Babb.

DEPARTURES

December 30, 1930. The snow begins falling a few minutes after 8:00 a.m., and the first callers arrive at the Bourgard residence on Remick Parkway in Lockport.

The Lockport merchants will be in a festive and generous mood today, their streetfront windows edged with glowing Christmas lights and promoting specialty items, such as Miller's fresh-dressed turkeys, ducks, geese, chickens, and 29-cent steaks, for New Year's Eve. Lucky indeed will be winner of the city's annual "New Year Baby" contest, for the merchants have already planned to shower down on the little one—the first baby born in 1931—"an avalanche of especially attractive and desirable gifts."

But none of this will be discussed at Emilie's funeral, which will begin at 8:30 at her home and continue at 9 o'clock at St. John's Church, where the Rev. Joseph Jacobs will attempt to shed some positive light on her passing.

Her mother, Eugenia, is still surprised. She expected to go first.

The callers ask about the black horse and Emilie's unfortunate accident. Poor thing, killed by her own carrousel. They are convinced of this, and the image provides a dramatic exit, which Emilie would have enjoyed.

She actually died of breast cancer, at 54.

They repeat the story for the benefit of the new arrivals and anyone who hasn't yet heard. It was late in the season, the carrousel now at Fort Niagara Beach, and Emilie was taking tickets on the ride, stepping between the jumping horses as it whirled, when one of the young riders dropped his ticket.

Above: Emilie Bourgard.

Page 58: Theo and Claire Morrot at Glen Park in 1932. Photos courtesy of the Morrot family.

When she stooped to pick it up, the knee of the black charger—the armored lead horse with the elegant plume—knocked her down. After that, she was never the same.

Poor thing, she died Saturday.

This is her husband, Pierre. We call him Peter.

This is her daughter, Philomina, and Philomina's husband, Leroy Ticer.

And this is Theophile—now Phil— her brother and business partner. They were always together. (What will he do without her?)

One thing he does is ponder the mystery of life and death and the feasibility of entering the priesthood, a vocation that has long attracted him. But, he concludes, it is too late for that. He is 40 years old, his mother is 79 and needs his support more than ever, and he has a contract to operate Emilie's carrousel at Fort Niagara Beach.

Whatever else he does, he does in a blur, remembering little.

He carries on despite the great emptiness.

He continues operating Emilie's carrousel as "a memorial to my sister, who designed it." Peter, a machinist at Harrison Radiator Company in Lockport, helps on weekends.

Now the 1931 season has closed, and the

The bereaved: Phil Morrot (left), Peter Bourgard (back), Leroy Ticer (right), and King. Emilie Bourgard was Phil's sister, Peter's wife, and Leroy's mother-in-law. Courtesy the Morrot family.

anniversary of Emilie's death draws near. Once again the Lockport merchants put up Christmas lights. Once again they advertise compelling New Year's Eve specials, and once again they plan for the annual New Year's Baby contest.

Theo resists the fresh grief that accompanies these innocent reminders. He decides to accept an invitation, and attends a New Year's Eve party.

And there she is, the delightful Claire Corona Trahan, a 30-year-old domestic from New Hampshire, who is visiting for the holidays.

He approaches her, smitten. "I waited a long time for her," he will one day tell his children. When it is time for Claire to return home, he will not allow it. "Send for your things," he tells her.

She does, and they are married on January 28, 1932, at St. Ann's Roman Catholic Church in Niagara Falls.

After the wedding, the bride moves into the Morrot family home, now a small house at 518 Prospect Street in Lockport, which is Eugenie's duchy. Claire's new mother-in-law makes a pretense of welcoming her, yet resents her presence, seizing every opportunity to demonstrate her influence over Phil.

But as Claire will tell her daughter, she was "wise to the old lady's tricks" and took equal pleasure in thwarting them. She will giggle as she describes how she fastened a piece of string in her hope chest to catch Eugenie snooping.

The next season opens with Emilie's carrousel in a new location, this time Glen Park in Williamsville, New York.

Glen Park is a beauty park bordering Ellicott Creek's popular waterfalls, with winding paths shaded by tall trees and rugged stone

Phil and Claire Morrot, their son, Paul, and King at Glen Park in Williamsville, N.Y. (1933). Courtesy, the Morrot family.

walls offering visitors an unobstructed view of the cascade. Phil operates Emilie's carrousel in Harry Altman's Glen Casino and Amusement Park complex. On the opposite bank are the stone foundations of old grist mills once powered by the waterfall.

Phil also operates a shooting gallery here. His is an entirely honest operation, but many customers find that hard to believe. One day a frustrated plinker challenges him, claiming the gallery guns are rigged. A skilled marksman, Phil relishes such occasions, for they allow him to put on a show: to settle the issue, he uses the gun in question to split playing cards, drive nails, and light matches.

It is no game, however, when a would-be burglar breaks a window at his Prospect Street home one evening and puts one leg inside. Phil, at the ready, takes silent aim with his loaded rifle. Just then Eugenie comes out of her bedroom calling, "Phil, is that you?"

This frightens the burglar, who escapes out the window.

With that saved life to her credit, Eugenie dies in July 1932 and is laid to rest next to Emilie, in St. Patrick's Cemetery in Lockport.

Phil and Claire's son, Paul, is born the following year, and Phil begins calling himself a regular family man.

An unidentified family on Emilie's carrousel at Glen Park. Note the double row of mirrors, with original oil paintings alternating between the mirrors. Courtesy Dan Wilke.

Paul Morrot on his mother's favorite horse. Courtesy the Morrot family.

According to Lockport city directories, Phil returns Emilie's carrousel to Fort Niagara Beach from 1933 to 1936, then moves it back to Glen Park from 1937 to 1939. At some point, the carrousel turns briefly at Sylvan Beach Park near Syracuse, New York.

Phil takes the pinto plane ride he purchased in 1935 with him to Glen Park. But the ride has one drawback—every time it rains, the planes hold water. That wasn't a problem at Fort Niagara Beach, where he tipped them upside down to drain. But at Glen Park, the guards were removing the planes from their chains and taking them down to the creek, where they had a grand time paddling around in them. Finally, Phil drills holes in all six of the planes to abort the mischief.

Phil's young son, Paul, also challenges him, by going in the water. Phil put an end to this by placing Paul in a harness and tying him to a tree.

In 1940, the carrousel circles back to its original location at Olcott Beach, where Phil manages the new Rialto Park.

The 1930s and '40s were prosperous decades for Olcott Beach. Big-band leaders such as Tommy and Jimmy Dorsey, Guy Lombardo, Artie Shaw, Charlie Barnet, Louis Armstrong, and Cab Calloway entertained crowds in the Olcott Beach Hotel and its outdoor music theaters. The hotel was razed in the 1930s to free up land for a new Niagara County park with picnic, playground, and sports areas, now known as Krull Park.

During the off season, Phil works at a foundry adjoining St. Patrick's Church and school in Lockport. Paul, who attends school there, has problems with his classmates—and especially a bully named Raymond—because he doesn't speak English; Phil and Claire speak French at home.

But Paul has an advantage.

Phil's window at the foundry looks out on the school yard, allowing him to keep an eye on Paul's activities there. Whenever

Phil, Claire, and Paul Morrot at Fort Niagara Beach. Note the streamlined elephant in the top photograph. Photographs courtesy the Morrot family.

the bullies start after Paul, he runs to his father's window—and before he gets there, the bullies give up the chase.

In 1940, after their daughter, Lucille, is born, Phil and Claire purchase a home and 14 acres of land along Tonawanda Creek in the hamlet of Indian Falls, New York.

His life now in order, Phil talks of owning his own park.

Above, right: Phil is getting in position to ride the rim of the Ferris wheel.

Below: One of the plane rides. Lucille Morrot (center) and her friends Joan, Polly, and Cleo. Photographs courtesy the Morrot family.

During the summer seasons, the Morrots and Uncle Pete (Emilie's husband) live in one of the small cottages behind the amusement area at Olcott Beach—a green cottage, the first in the line.

It was at Olcott Beach that Phil first rode the rim of the Ferris wheel. "The guy that operated the Ferris wheel for Flynn got to be friends with my dad. And one night, my dad and this guy were competing to see how many times they could ride the rum without touching the ground," recalls Paul Morrot.

"Father went around some 20 times, and then his hands got sweaty. He started slipping as he got halfway up and had to let go.

"When he fell, he came down straddling the white picket fence around the ride, and tore his pants. As the Ferris wheel kept turning, he ran to the cottage and changed his pants, then ran back and unloaded it—it was full of passengers.

The attraction that caused the greatest stir at Olcott Beach, however, was the mouse game, with live mice.

"The game was a table with holes around the outside edge, each hole a different color, Paul explains. "The board was also painted in different colors, and people would put their money on a color.

"The mice were under a box on the table. We'd raise

Below: Two of the Olcott Beach cottages still stand. The Morrot family and Uncle Pete lived in one during the summer seasons; Lucille Morrot believes it was the cottage on the left. Photograph by Cyndy Hanks, 2003.

the box and let them out, and whatever color hole the mouse went in, the person who picked that color won.

"We let the people shout and make noise to affect which hole the mouse went in, but the New York State Police ruled that it was gambling, destroyed the game, and arrested the mouse man.

"The mouse man won a lawsuit for damages to his property and was compensated, but with the understanding that he would never open the mouse game again. The police told my dad if he reopened the mouse game, they would arrest him every time.

"The Lions Club liked to borrow the lion for parades," Paul continues. "So we'd run the merry-go-round without it. We never had much trouble. Sometimes wise guys would climb on the animals, using the giraffe's horns for handles—we had to repair it several times."

Above: The popular mouse game at Olcott Beach.

Below: A local band plays as the Ferris wheel turns. Photographs courtesy the Morrot family.

Lee Ticer, Philomina's husband, was Olcott Beach's fire chief; they lived across the street from the fire department.

One evening the sirens went off, and Paul walked down to the park. A man who was riding the rim had fallen from the top and hit a hard park bench. The impact literally knocked the soles off his shoes.

"He had brown shoes," recalls Paul. "His shoes were still on his feet, but the soles were off to the side. An ambulance from Wrights Corners came and took him to the hospital. He survived, and I saw him a couple years later, walking with two canes. After that, whenever Father rode the rim, I would yell at him and threaten to shut down the ride.

"But Father didn't stop until he broke his skull. Then he never did it again. But he *thought about it* a couple times. . . ."

On December 7, 1941, shortly before his 61st birthday, Phil hears the news: "The Japanese have attacked Pearl Harbor, the United States naval base on Oahu Island in the Hawaiian Islands."

The following day, Congress declares war on Japan. Idle factories all over the country spring into full production, and even busy factories convert their machinery for wartime use. Roosevelt promised the Allies 60,000 planes a year—an astounding figure at the time—and the factory workers labor to prove him right.

These skilled hands belong to 65-year-old Herman Jagow, who used to turn out merry-go-round horses to gladden the hearts of the nation's children. Here he is doing lathe work for landing gear housings for the dread Airacobra pursuit ship. Spillman Engineering Company, North Tonawanda, New York (1942). Courtesy Library of Congress.

As the 1942 season opens at Olcott Beach, a team of scientists at Los Alamos steps up work on the atomic bomb, not knowing if it will ever go off, or even if it does, if they can control the reaction.

Phil again adapts to the requirements of war, working at Curtis-Wright as a machinist. He uses his ration stamps for gasoline for the tractor engine that runs the Ferris wheel, as he could not afford to lose the income.

Then on July 16, 1945, there is a tremendous explosion of light over the city of Hiroshima, in Japan. An inferno of flames is dwarfed by a rising column of smoke that gradually balloons into an enormous mushroom-shaped cloud. World War II is over.

After the war, the decline in tourism continues, and businesses struggle to survive. Phil attempts to buy the Olcott Beach amusement area, but the owner will not hear of it.

He continues to manage the operation, but only after negotiating his own terms. The canvas top on the merry-go-round is wearing out, he tells the owner. The ride should be inside a building. He is willing to construct a building, but it will belong to him—and should he ever decide to leave, it goes with him.

As the story goes, the owner thought Phil was bluffing and doubted he would ever move the building—and she signed the agreement.

Then, Paul said, "Once the merry-go-round building was completed, she raised the percentage of her take from 15 to 20 percent.

"Father said, 'If you do that, I'm moving out. I have a family to feed.'" But she will not relent, so his father walks away.

But soon he is back with a saw. Working methodically, he saws the building into sections, stacking them on the ground. Then he loads the sections and other wood onto his truck. (He had traded his 2.5-ton Chevy truck for a GMC lumber company truck large enough carry the entire seven-ton Ferris wheel in one trip.)

He took the load to Indian Falls, where the family now lived, and stored it in an old mill on his property. Next he disassembled the carrousel, the Ferris wheel, the pinto plane ride, the kiddie auto ride, and everything else that belonged to him, and moved them all to Indian Falls.

Well before he arrived with the first load, however, Phil decided to build his own park.

Above: King and Phil on the Ferris wheel.

Below: Paul and Phil with Emilie's carrousel at Olcott Beach, sans building. Photographs courtesy the Morrot family.

Above: A Sunday School picnic at Indian Falls in the 1920s.

Left: Augustus ("Gus") Meiser, in his eighties. What kept Gus going was his hatred for weeds. He spent nearly all his time in his potato field, hoeing. When eventually his legs failed, Gus moved his yellow wooden chair out into the field, where, seated, he would hoe as far as he could reach. Then he'd stand, move the chair forward, sit down, and again hoe as far as he could reach. Once when visiting a neighbor, Gus looked out the window and saw weeds choking the neighbor's field. "I have to go. I'm feeling sick," he said, and left. Photographs courtesy Town of Pembroke historian.

INDIAN FALLS

May 1, 1949. Today, May Day, in the tiny hamlet of Indian Falls, New York. A handful of children who live here pause at the edge of the ravine before swooping down to pick the wild violets, bluebells, and white trillium growing on its shady damp incline and floor. The trilliums are also called Wake Robin, as they appear every spring when the robins return.

This is an annual custom. Soon the children will hand deliver their sweet wildflower baskets to mothers, aunts, and favorite neighbor ladies, giggling with pleasure at the recipients' profuse gratitude. The gratitude is heartfelt, as the men of Indian Falls, most of them hard-working farmers, are largely unaware of the importance of flowers and the women's yearning for them, which the children enthusiastically allay. The mutual joy perpetuates the custom and has already taught the children the blessedness of giving.

These are quick, resourceful children, whose days are filled with the delight of discovery. They amuse themselves, and they appear content wherever they are, whether it's playing in a sandbox, clustered together at family picnics, skipping down

the dirt road connecting their respective homes, walking straight through the cow pasture, or digging in the cornfields for arrowheads and fossils. Later this year they will make hollyhock dolls, snack on wild elderberries, and catch mudpuppies.

They live happily in a time warp, ten years behind the times, and in no particular hurry to catch up. Relics of the past are

Above: Paul and Lucille Morrot. Courtesy the Morrot family.

Below: Tonawanda Creek, looking toward the Route 77 bridge and the "big falls." Courtesy Town of Pembroke Historian.

The Tonawanda Band of Senecas "All Indian Band" at the Akron Band Stand, July 4, 1922. Seated, left to right: Howard Pierce, Norman Parker, Ira Mitten, Sr., and Nick Bailey. Second row, left to right: Harrison Ground, Robert Shanks, Ben Ground, and Raymond Moses. Back row, left to right: Delbert Moses, Barnum Poodry, Hiram Moses, James C. Skye, Jessie Hill, Freeman Johnson, McRay Skye, Owen Skye, Seaver Blackchief, Marvin Cook, and Heman Doctor. One name is missing for this picture. Courtesy John L. Eckerson.

Ely S. Parker, born in Indian Falls when it was part of the Tonawanda Reservation. Courtesy Pembroke Historical Society.

included in their present: abandoned wagon wheels edge their ample lawns, their hand-crank telephones share a party line, and old Vern Fenner still uses his outhouse. Occasionally a bobcat makes its presence known during the night, snarling from the woods along the Tonawanda Reservation, but otherwise the children sleep to the lullabies of tree frogs, crickets, and cicada.

The inhabitants of the reservation, the Tonawanda Band of Senecas, attend the local schools, serve as U.S. soldiers, help deliver and care for the community's newborns, and provide their marching bands and ceremonial dances for neighborhood events, their performers in full headdress.

Although none of these children are descendents of the Senecas, they have absorbed some of the Indian culture. They walk the same soil as White Chief and past generations of Iroquois warriors did, for Indian Falls was part of the reservation until 1857. Its northern portion was the site of an Indian village and a source of flint for arrowheads for the Senecas and the entire Iroquois Confederacy—and once belonged to the parents of Ely S. Parker, the hamlet's most famous celebrity.

Parker, the son of William and Elizabeth Parker (William was a U.S. Army veteran of the War of 1812, the first of 600 Senecas to enroll), was born in a log cabin overlooking the "big falls," then part of the Tonawanda Reservation. He volunteered into the army, became General Grant's military secretary, and helped draft the final terms of the Confederate surrender at Appomattox in 1865. (President Grant appointed him the first Commissioner of Indian Affairs on April 13, 1869.)

News of a new park was reported as early as January 26, 1949, when the *Batavia Daily News* ran an article under the headline, "Theo Morrot to Build Park."

The article said that Theo Morrot, owner of the former Reynolds farm and feed mill on Phelps Road, would open "Boulder Park" on Memorial Day, May 28, and hoped to have it ready on weekends before then.

Boulder Park, it said, would offer at least five rides: a merry-go-round, a Ferris wheel, a kiddie auto ride, an airplane ride, and kiddie chairplanes, all owned by Morrot, and that he was making arrangements for a pony ride and miniature train, as well as games, refreshment stands, snack tents, and wading pools for younger children.

The heart of Indian Falls, where six Indian trails once met. A double-arch concrete bridge replaced the iron bridge in 1927. The entrance to Boulder Park will be on Phelps Road, just before the intersection, at the base of the bridge. Courtesy Town of Pembroke Historian.

For nine years now, the Morrots have lived in a wood frame house on Phelps Road, their back lawn a bluff overlooking the new park site. They regularly attend services at the Catholic church in nearby Corfu, participate in social events at the Indian Falls Methodist Church, and are considered "a nice family."

The site Phil Morrot selected for Boulder Park is at the heart of Indian Falls, "between two great hills in the narrow valley of the Tonnewanta"—now called Tonawanda Creek— and the site where six Indian trails once met. The park entrance is on Phelps Road at the foot of the double-arch concrete bridge. A picnic grove and amusements will populate the broad strip of land along the north bank of the creek.

Authors have long described Indian Falls as a well-hidden "fairy spot, blessed by God and nature"—so richly blessed, that in 1924, Ely S. Parker's grandson, New York State archaeologist Arthur C. Parker, enthusiastically endorsed a proposal by New York Senator Nathan Strauss, Jr., to preserve its beauty for public use as a state park.

The old Gillmore Mill on Gillmore Road; the property included the "big falls" cascade. Courtesy Town of Pembroke Historian.

Above the bridge, the stream in a series of tiny rapids curves from behind the foliage of its wooded shores, slips through a channel choked with huge rocks, and comes to pause in a deep pool. The waters are halted by an ancient, worn-out wooden dam under the bridge, from which it emerges as a silvery surface studded with boulders. Then it glides away in glistening splendor to the roaring cascade a hundred yards in the distance.

"Willows and frail undergrowth arch gracefully over the edge of the creek. On the right bank, looking downstream, is a hill crowned with tall elms, aromatic pines, and dignified chestnut trees. On this hill is a large grove that is a favorite with picnickers, and from it an excellent view of the Falls can be had. Curling around multitudes of large, flat rocks, the water becomes more and more turbulent as it nears the brink of the waterfall, where as though resigned to its fate, it hurls itself over in a double cascade 35 feet in height. The water does not take a direct plunge, but splashes from rock to rock, churning itself into a creamy splendor.

"In places the creek seeps through tiny crevices in the rock, and all the trickling, dripping, and falling waters are united below in a big deep pool that whirls dizzily around before it straightens out to hurry through innumerable boulders along the gorge. Vines and bushes cling to the brink of the cascade and to the ledges above and below it. An old wooden mill stands, like the ghost of the years past, on one side of the waterfall. Songbirds fly back and forth, but their chirps are drowned out by the everlasting roar of the water.

"Descent into the gorge may be made by means of a gloomy, slippery path. Down here the sun bathes the stream and dull stones in a radiance of light. The trees stretch heavenward as though to intercept the rays of the sun.

"Downstream, the creek soon curves from sight, beyond the bend. But only another curve is seen; the waters wind their way mysteriously from view. All about are signs of countless picnics and corn roasts. Ever in the ears is the roar of the falls, blending with the rush of the rapids.

—Batavia Daily News, *January 17, 1924*

"I am especially interested, because my grandfather at one time owned the place," Parker commented then. "People gravitate to it and have done so for years. It's a case of the people going there, and not one of making a park and saying to the people: 'Here's a park; now go to it.'" He recommended the proposal be included in a large appropriation for a number of park sites, to improve its chances of approval by Governor Smith.

But there was one problem: the Falls proposal received so much publicity that its owner set his price too high.

"He seems to think he has a goldmine," Parker commented.

Assemblyman Charles P. Miller and others tried every method to get the owner of the cascade to set a reasonable price on his land, which included the old mill. But he resisted, holding out for the right to conduct a hot dog stand there following the state's approval.

Commissioner Humphrey suggested the state tear down the mill, build steps leading to the gorge below the cascade, and purchase the strip of land connecting Tonawanda Creek with Diver's Lake—which would make the park area horseshoe-shaped.

The president of the state Association for Constructive Legislation and Responsible and Economical Government enthusiastically endorsed the acquisition, saying, "This beauty spot should be owned by the state, for the benefit of its people, but it should be left as near a state of nature as possible, that people may

About a half-mile up the road, north of the big falls, is Diver's Lake (named for its original white owner, Edward Diver), also known as Devil's Lake, Spirit Lake (the Senecas believed the spirit sea serpent Sais-Tah-Go-Wah lived there), Indian Pond, Hidden Lake, Bottomless Lake, and Dead Lake. The spring-fed lake is well hidden from the road, in a thick grove of oak, maple, and silver-barked birch trees, and an occasional pine.

The mothers and fathers of Indian Falls know how to find it, but they do not share this information with their children, instead cautioning them to forget even trying to find the evil lake, which has already stolen lives and property. Nonetheless, some of the children sneak there regularly.

"A path through a magnificent woods leads the visitor to it," wrote a local author in 1925. "Squirrels dart across the shadowy land and overhead crows caw lazily as they flap slowly away. A side path leads to the edge of a stone cliff a hundred feet high. The ravine is filled with great trees, through which one finally gains a view of the little lake. A path roofed with a rocky shelf follows along the face of the cliff, and another path takes one sharply down to the lake."

Diver's Lake has been the subject of many strange tales. Some say it has no bottom in the middle, and that it has a subterranean inlet and outlet. Others say its bottom near the shore is quicksand, "into which an object sinks as though it were falling into a cloud."

Years ago, ancestors of the Senecas told of dead flat fish floating to the lake's surface, squashed by the high pressure of the deep waters in which they lived. The fish had no eyes, they said, because they lived in dark underground streams.

Diver's Lake. Courtesy Town of Pembroke Historian.

73

Almond and Orr's general store in Indian Falls, New York. The building still stands today.

Below: Phil Morrot purchased this house in Indian Falls for rental income. The lower level had a dirt floor and room for three cars, the first floor was a store, and he added two apartments on the second floor. Courtesy Town of Pembroke historian.

picnic there in the future very much as they have in the past. Improvements should be only of an incidental character necessary to keep things in a state of nature, with walks . . . so they can be enjoyed."

With so much support for the idea, the community assumed the state would purchase the land soon.

"The only thing supporters of the project think likely to hold up favorable action by the state is the attempt by the owner of the Falls to get too high a price for his property," said Parker. "The owner of Diver's Lake . . . is willing to sell at a reasonable figure."

The owner of the cascade property literally held his ground, however, and the state park never materialized.

The former creamery, another failed dream, was now a vacant structure on the Boulder Park site.

"A tragic sight, to see ravaged by rust and dirt the valuable apparatus installed in a modern creamery a few years ago when farmers thought the road to wealth lay through organization of a co-operative dairy company to purchase their milk and manufacture butter on the spot," penned journalist Marjorie Marble, for the *Buffalo Evening News*, sometime around 1925.

"That flourished a few years, and the investors dreamed of big dividends as soon as all the debts were paid, but about that time, the dairy business began to hit the skids, and for nearly 15 years the creamery has lain idle, except for storage purposes."

Without a healthy industry to replace its defunct milling operations and creamery, Indian Falls slid into a decline.

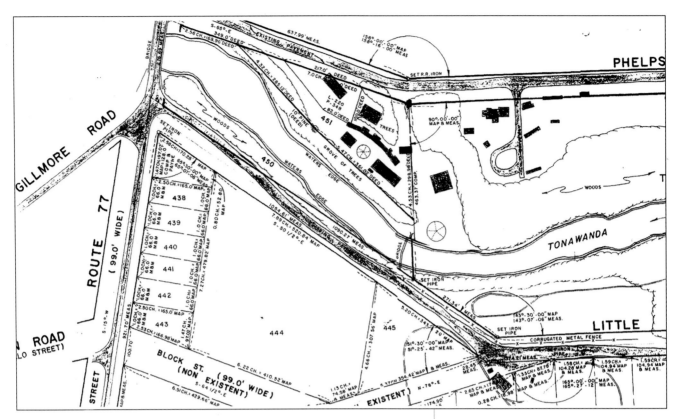

The Boulder Park site. The Morrots lived on Phelps Road, above the park site. They added a large parking area and a trailer court there. Courtesy the Morrot family.

In 1928, Marble despaired, "Except for the farm changes in surrounding countryside, the family names on the letter boxes remain the same from generation to generation. Now and then there is some starved soul who seeks an education . . . and then what is the use? . . . one doesn't need Greek and Latin to run a farm."

During World War II, however, the community proved its mettle. Some residents headed up Defense Bond drives in nearby towns, while others acted as plane spotters for the U.S. Army.

Even farmers who put in a full day on their farms worked the night shift in defense plants. The women, too, took jobs in the plants, and even the children pitched in—when a request was issued for milkweed floss to take the place of kapok, for example, the 4-H boys and girls produced many bags of the pods for the war effort.

The cows, however, were another story. When in February 1942 all clocks were turned ahead an hour for the duration of the war, they balked, refusing to arise until they were ready.

The one-room schoolhouse on Alleghany Road (Route 77), where most of the Indian Falls residents learned their ABCs. It was later converted to a home, but retains much of its outside appearance today. Courtesy Town of Pembroke historian.

Above: An aerial view of Boulder Park. The bingo hall is in front. Behind it are the creamery building, which was converted to a restaurant, and the apple dryer building, which was used as an office and for storage. The kiddie rides are to the right of the concession buildings and include (front to back) the Allan Herschell boat ride, two chair-plane rides, and an auto ride (under the shelter). Behind the Ferris wheel is Emilie's carrousel; the path away from the carrousel leads up the bank to a large parking area and the Morrot family's home (the Morrots added a trailer court later). The building on the right was Pratt's mill. Courtesy Paul Morrot.

BOULDER AMUSEMENT PARK

Finally Memorial Day, May 28, 1949. Phil Morrot flips the switch on the Wurlitzer military band organ, and a foreign but merry sound intrudes upon the Indian Falls community, commanding its immediate attention.

The sound is nearly as loud as that of the bells in the Indian Falls Methodist Church steeple—and equally effective, bringing a sudden halt to all activity.

The merry music has done its job; the children come to life first. They begin marching in time, conducting in time, bouncing their pets in time, waving their popsicles in time, digging their sand shovels in time. Next, the women begin stirring in time, stepping in time, waving their hair brushes in time. And then the men join in—at first merely humming and tapping, but soon their feet and hands, as well, are moving; it is a spontaneous community performance, full of energy. The heart of Indian Falls is beating again, pumping life into its inhabitants.

As another invigorating melody begins, the realization hits: Boulder Park is not waiting for us to visit, it has already arrived—and its pied piper music is working.

The new park is enthusiastically received by the Indian Falls community, and on June 2, *The Daily News* reports: "Theo Morrot has opened the new Boulder Park. There was a large attendance on Memorial Day."

Word spreads quickly, and soon hundreds of automobiles, many from as far away as Buffalo and Rochester and Olcott Beach—fill the parking area, a large, graded field on Phelps Road, near the Morrot family's home.

The Morrots' property covers 14 acres, including their home, a five-acre orchard, the six-acre field used for parking,

Top: Attention in the sandbox! Everything stopped when the merry-go-round music began. Author's collection.

Above: The footbridge over Tonawanda Creek leading into Boulder Park from the opposite side. Courtesy Town of Pembroke historian.

and the land between Phelps Road and Tonawanda Creek, the site of Boulder Park.

Back when Phil heard the property was for sale, he was financially strapped. Raising a family, albeit a small one, was becoming increasingly difficult with the declining park attendance, so he borrowed the money from an electrician in Lockport, closing the deal in April 1940.

The property was described as two water power lots "on Tonawanda Creek, with the mill erected thereon [Pratt's mill], with all machinery and implements used in and about said mill [and additional acreage]. All of the above described premises are a part of the Tonawanda Reservation and 12,800 acre tract, and are distinguished on a map of the Village plot by made by Jerome Carey [1843], and the tracts above described contain 12.71 and 1.62 acres respectively [formerly known as the Reynolds farm]." In October 1945, Phil and Claire also purchased the defunct Indian Falls Creamery Company, bringing the total acreage to 14.

Although Phil has owned the property for eight years, it is still undeveloped in 1948 when he decides to build his park there. According to his son, Paul, Phil was always working on their house.

Above: The entrance to the park offered few parking spots. When the spots up front and in the picnic area were filled, families parked in a large field on Phelps Road, then walked on stone steps down the creekbank to the amusement area below, coming out near the Ferris wheel and merry-go-round. Courtesy the Morrot family.

Visitors descend the stone steps from the parking lot above, past the apple dryer and merry-go-round buildings, down to the Ferris wheel and midway. Courtesy the Morrot family.

"When we moved there—in the fall—the house was in bad shape," Paul says. "My father had to do a lot of work to make it livable. He dug out a cellar so he could install a coal furnace, and when he was working down there, I talked to him through the cracks in the floor."

It takes Phil several months to clear the land and remove the trees and undergrowth along the creek, his progress impeded by the many boulders on the site. Boulders cover the creekbed, and boulders rise out of the water like giant lilypads—in some places forming a walkway to the other side. Boulders have stacked up at the edge of the creek, crept up the creekbank, and now squat on the land above. One boulder (a pinkish color), described by Paul as "about twice the size of a refrigerator on the bottom," sits right where Phil wants to place the Ferris wheel.

Turning disadvantage to advantage, he touts the boulders as an attraction and names his park "Boulder Park."

Today he will take Paul to the Tonawanda Reservation, to select a slippery elm tree for the "greasy pole."

Nearly everyone who lived in Indian Falls worked at Boulder Park or was touched by the park in some way. Here, some favorite ladies serve up snacks and refreshments. Courtesy the Morrot family.

Climbing a greasy pole is very difficult, Phil explains, despite the simplicity of the challenge. Once stripped of its bark, the naturally slimy tree will defy all contenders. Soon countless men—shirtless and sweaty in their coveralls—will place one determined hand above the other, reaching higher and higher, even as they slip to the ground. Some will form a human pyramid to give the topmost man an advantage. But even this will not work.

Pratt's mill, more historic than useful, also squats on the property. But since it is historic, Phil repairs its roof and uses it for storage and as a workshop.

He installs toilets in the apple dryer building, which has thick, concrete walls, and begins construction on the merry-go-round building—which replaces the old apple processing building.

While the merry-go-round building is under construction, he puts canvas around the ride, dropping it to the ground at night to protect the figures.

"My first job in the morning was to roll up the canvas," Paul explains. "I'd start at one place and start rolling it, and when I got to the top, there were straps built into the canvas, and I would strap it. When the ride operated, there was a draping of canvas all around,

Above: Phil is a familiar figure at the Ferris wheel, as he was its primary operator. The ride was a #5 Big Eli® wheel manufactured in 1921 by the Eli Bridge Company (serial number 254). As the riders passed the park's cherry tree, children would pick and eat the cherries. Phil built the ticket booth at Olcott Beach. It had two windows—one for the Ferris wheel tickets, and the other for the manager. Courtesy the Lennon family.

Page 82, left: A view of the Ferris wheel and Pratt's mill. The "greasy pole" can be seen in front of the mill building. Courtesy the Morrot family.

Page 82, top: The girl in the middle, in pigtails, is Lucille Morrot, Phil's daughter. Courtesy the Morrot family.

right beneath the cornice. My mother sewed all the canvas for the park on her heavy old Singer sewing machine with a foot pedal."

Phil hauls in crushed stone for the entrance, midway, and ride areas. He builds a  footbridge over the creek and a shelter for the kiddie auto ride. He hires Herb Barker to build concession stands with the wood from the dismantled merry-go-round building. Herb is meticulous; they are like cabinets.

Boulder Park was an immediate sensation that lasted nearly two decades, bringing enjoyment, employment, and tourism to Indian Falls. Photographs courtesy the Morrot family.

He installs electric service, signs contracts with vendors, and orders signs, tickets, matchbooks, light bulbs, and other necessities. He places the main ticket booth near the Ferris wheel and puts heavy wood picnic tables in the grove beside the creek.

Then, in January 1949, Phil starts running ads in *The Daily News.*

"Boulder Park. Indian Falls, N.Y. on Route 77. Bring this coupon and 25¢ to Boulder Park and get 50¢ worth of ride tickets for children under 12 years."

"Free Admission, Plenty of Free Parking."

"All kiddie rides 5 cents."

Boulder Park offers six rides: a merry-go-round, a Ferris wheel, a kiddie auto ride, two chair-plane rides, and a new Allan Herschell kiddie boat ride. Paul believes the boat ride was the company's first, a prototype his father tested for John Wendler. Phil and John are good friends, and Phil will test other rides for him in the future.

Even with the success of opening day, Phil continues to work the community, anticipating its distractions and diverting them.

Lest its constituency forget the park is open, the carrousel's penetrating band organ gives ample warning. At noon, Phil sends its pied piper melodies soaring through the air to every individual within earshot, some nearly a mile away. The catchy music continues until 1 p.m., when the park officially opens.

In a matter of weeks and despite its remote location, Boulder Park is packed with people and keeps at least a dozen workers and Phil's children busy. Phil operates the Ferris wheel and occasionally sells tickets. Uncle Pete operates the carrousel during the week, and Claire runs it Sundays and holidays. Most of the other workers are the park's Indian Falls neighbors.

Phil takes extra measures to protect Emilie's carrousel, installing overhead doors on the new building. He requests special tracks and springs to ensure the doors clear the ride's outside cornice. But this solution has a drawback—enclosing the building will make the carrousel a dark ride. So he has a row of windows installed at the roofline, in the same style as those on its peak.

Above: Paul Morrot on the kiddie car ride. Shown here at Olcott Beach, Phil brought this ride with him to Indian Falls. It was two rides in one, running with either 10 cars or eight, to save space. Phil first used this ride in Cleveland in the railroad tower. While there, he paid 50 cents for a raffle ticket and won a Rolls Royce pedal car, which was Paul's Christmas present that year. Courtesy the Morrot family.

Below: Down the path to the merry-go-round and Ferris wheel. Courtesy the Morrot family.

Above: Boulder Park became a much larger community than Indian Falls, in terms of numbers of people per square foot. Courtesy the Lennon family.

Below: A view of Boulder Park from the opposite side of Tonawanda Creek. Paul built the chair swing ride, which whirled passengers out over the water. The park also offered archery for the Senecas, and had Senecas from the Tonawanda Reservation run it. Next to the archery area was an Indian souvenir stand. Courtesy the Morrot family.

Seemingly overnight, a transformation has taken place. Previously sedentary individuals have become high-energy entrepreneurs, selling their own hand-made souvenirs and running clever games and concessions. And the park has become a festive melting pot, engaging all kinds of people in a grand endeavor that is more satisfying than war production, and infinitely more pleasant. And so they give it their full energy.

Boulder Park is open daily during the summer from 1 p.m. to 11 p.m., and Paul and Lucille are among the hardest workers. But their work begins in the morning, well before the park opens. They sprinkle water on the midway to control the dust, and they dust all the rides. They also dust the merry-go-round figures, grease its poles and joints, and sweep the platform with a push-broom, among other chores.

"We worked in the park every single day," Lucille recalls. "We'd work and work and work and work, and six o'clock would come and then seven o'clock, and it was still daylight, so Father would send Paul down to Passmore's store for four pints of ice cream, and that would be our dinner. He'd say, 'And make sure they give you the wooden spoons.' "

Passmore's store—set up in the left half of Elmer Passmore's small home—was an event unto itself.

"What a place," laughs Paul.

"You'd go in the door, and if you went straight, you'd end up in their living room.

Left: The building on the left is the new bingo shelter, built after the fire in the creamery building. It was enclosed and turned into a storage facility after New York State shut down all gambling operations. The creamery building is in back. Courtesy the Morrot family.

"They hung a curtain there, to separate it from the store. The main counter was split, too, with shelves of groceries on the left, and a little counter where Mrs. Passmore took your money. The store wasn't any wider than 12 feet. One day my dad sent me down to get a loaf of bread; bread was maybe 12 cents a loaf then.

"When I went down the hill, I saw this cat cross the road. And when I came back, the cat was at the bottom of the hill, and I kind of liked the cat, so I picked it up by the tail—and I'm carrying the loaf of bread in one hand and the cat in the other, walking up the hill.

"I thought it was funny that two or three cars drove down past me as this was going on, and the drivers blew their horns and waved at me, sideways. I wondered, 'What the heck,' but I took the cat home and laid it under an old washtub, and went in the house.

"When I walked in, my dad was sitting at the breakfast table, and I gave my mother the bread. And my dad said, 'Where the *hell* have you *been*?'

"I looked at him kind of funny, and he said, 'You have been with a skunk.'

"My mother made me take my clothes off, outside on the back porch, and my dad took a stick and made the skunk go. They asked, 'What did you think that smell *was*?' But apparently I hadn't noticed it. I hadn't been out in the country very long."

An early photo of Passmore's store, which appeared pretty much the same through the 1950s. Courtesy Town of Pembroke historian.

Now Phil is planning a big event—Boulder Park's first Indian Field Day on August 20. The event will be well attended, for the Tonawanda Senecas are looking forward to entertaining a crowd, and the community is looking forward to their entertainment—a lacrosse game, a baseball game, and an Indian Band concert with ceremonial dances, the performers in full headdress.

But the event has a greater purpose than mere entertainment; Phil is doing everything in his power to stay a step ahead of the next bogey. The bogey is watching, watching, patiently waiting for him to let down his guard. To Phil, it is not a matter of *if* it will strike, but *when*.

So, vigilant, he watches, too. And listens.

June 11 got off to a slow start, he noted, because many people were dallying in front of new televisions, captive to the day's news: "A crowded court docket might delay for a year the trial of auto maker Preston T. Tucker and his associates on federal charges for promoting a rear-engine automobile."

To make matters worse, Phil also noted, newspaper reporters are predicting that color television may arrive in Genesee County next year.

"Don't be idle," he cautions Paul and Lucille.

On July 1, *The Daily News* reports two newsworthy developments—a drowning tragedy the previous day at Indian Falls, and "Genesee Drive-In Theater Opening Tomorrow."

Perhaps this time it will be a double bogey.

BOULDER PARK
Indian Falls, N. Y., Rte. 77

On the banks of Tonawanda Creek. Plenty of Free Parking. Opened every day 1 P. M. on. Picnic Groves, Tables and Fireplaces.

On Aug. 20th Indian Field Day
LaCross Game, Ball Game
Indian Band Concert.

Phil's ad in The Daily News. *Author's collection.*

Below: The captivating and memorable Tonawanda Reservation Band. This photograph was taken in September 1953. The band has long participated in parades and events in its neighboring communities. Courtesy John L. Eckerson.

The drownings are a tragic but familiar event for Indian Falls residents. Every year city boys arrive in their cars to challenge the falls, diving from its high rock ledge into the turbulent water below, ignoring the hand-lettered sign tacked to the big tree on the south bank: "No Swimming. Danger. Undertow."

Almost every year, one or more of the daredevils drown.

The drowning victims share a common experience; they are greatly surprised when they are sucked into the powerful eddy. Some never surface until their bodies appear on the Tonawanda Reservation or are pulled from Diver's Lake. Others emerge only after hours of dragging with grappling hooks, a sad and unpleasant ritual for the local police, firemen, and volunteers.

This time *two* young men have drowned, both of them local boys. They are Lester Conibear, a volunteer fireman, and Daniel Kocol, a construction worker at the State School for the Blind in Batavia, both 20, and Kokol an expert swimmer! They are recovered at the foot of the falls, one from a hole about 40 feet deep near the south bank, the other the following day in about 15 feet of water near the north bank.

Conibear is mourned as a hero. Still wearing his trousers and socks, he plunged in the water to save his friend—and it sucked him in, too.

The day after the drownings, all the mothers who read the grim article question the wisdom of taking their children anywhere near the murderous creek.

But Sunday at noon, they dismiss these thoughts when the bells in the Indian Falls Methodist Church steeple announce—this time with "Rock of Ages"—that the service is over, and the merry-go-round music begins. By the time one o'clock arrives, even the unruliest children are dressed and ready to go.

Local police, firemen, and volunteers use grappling hooks to drag Tonawanda Creek for drowning victims. Most of the dragging operations took place during the summer, but this macabre scene happened when school was in session. It was viewed with interest by children as their schoolbus traveled over the Route 77 bridge. Courtesy the Morrot family.

Tonawanda Creek, above the falls. The young men who drowned at Indian Falls on June 30, 1949 were found at the base of the falls. The bodies of some drowning victims, however, did not surface until they reached Diver's Lake or the Tonawanda Reservation. Courtesy the Morrot family.

Boulder Park has a heyday in the 1950s. Some weekends, more than 900 cars fill the parking field, and a constant stream of visitors descends the stone steps to Emilie's carrousel.

Yet Phil takes nothing for granted. He remains in constant motion.

"Dad was *always* working." Lucille recalls. "If he *did* come in the house to rest, he would sit in front of the TV. Before the TV, it was the radio. Sometimes we'd play Chinese checkers or put together puzzles, or I'd play piano for them, or I'd be in the kitchen, baking with my mother.

"But usually, if Dad wasn't working at the park, he'd be working in the yard or on the property—weeding, picking up rocks, cutting wood, and trimming. When he had a garden, he worked in the garden until dark. He was never idle."

Top: The Little Dipper roller coaster. Courtesy the Morrot family.

Above: During the 1950s, many merchants capitalized on the popularity of merry-go-rounds. Author's collection.

Right: Route 77 has earned its "snowbelt" reputation. Winter storms often dumped several feet of snow on Indian Falls, but spared areas to the east and west. Heavy snow was responsible for collapsing the the kiddie auto ride shelter—and the roof of the merry-go-round building, which crushed the ride. Courtesy the Morrot family.

It was in the late 1950s that the merry-go-round building collapsed under the weight of a heavy snow, crushing the ride.

"Fortunately, we had it fixed by spring, but it took all winter to get the work done," said Paul. "We were lucky there was no damage to the inside panels, mirrors, and paintings. We always took them down in the fall and stored them, covered, in the center of the machine."

Phil turns the creamery building into a restaurant, which fails—and then a bingo hall, which is a big success. But then the bingo hall burns, and eventually New York State shuts down the operation altogether.

"That was a big loss," recalls Paul, "because the man who ran the bingo hall didn't skimp on prizes. He had expanded into the building in the back, so people could sit in either building and play the same game, while listening to the speakers."

Occasionally gypsies would come through Indian Falls in wagons, looking for a place to camp. (Most likely, they were the Rusniakuria, or Ruthenians, a subset of the Rom, from Serbia, Russia, and Austria-Hungary.)

"My father would set them up in the parking lot," Paul relates. "They were fortune-tellers, and they had singers and musicians. One morning, when I was cleaning the park, one of the women started talking to me. She offered to tell my fortune and not charge anything. So I went in there, and although she said a lot of things, the only thing that stuck with me was that I was in uniform, and my parents would be proud of me.

"Normally the way they operated, the women would tell fortunes to hold the attention of the community, and the men would be roaming around, say, Corfu or Batavia or Clarence or Basom—all around here, but never where their camp was. But I don't remember any problems with them."

Eventually, however, despite its reputation as a family park that did not allow liquor or tolerate rowdiness, Boulder Park began to attract troublemakers.

"First we had trouble with people from Buffalo who had been drinking. They got on the Ferris wheel and were rocking the seat back and forth so bad, they almost flipped it.

"Then they got on the merry-go-round and stood on the horses, and started jumping from horse to horse. So we shut down the ride and told them to leave the park. They even threatened my dad," Paul recalls.

"We had called the police as soon as the trouble started, but they never came until we were closing the park. So the next day, Father and I traded his steel-barrel shotgun for a Winchester pump, the shortest legal barrel he could get for a scatter gun, and we kept it in the park.

"Because it was only Father and me, and troublemakers are capable of a lot of damage, I became a constable in 1954. Two years later, I became a state trooper—just in case we had more problems."

Left to right: An unidentified customer, Phil, and Paul wih Emilie's carrousel. Note the fluorescent lights that Phil has added inside the ride. Courtesy the Morrot family.

When bands of gypsies came through Indian Falls, Phil would set them up in the parking lot. Author's collection.

When trouble started, the park needed help quickly.
So Paul Morrot, 23, became a constable, and in
1956, a New York State trooper, to maintain order.
He was assisted by Johnny Adams, an Indian Falls
resident and Genesee County deputy. This is Paul's
1955 Ford patrol car. Courtesy the Morrot family.

THE DAILY NEWS.

BATAVIA, N. Y., FRIDAY, JULY 31, 1959

WARDEN AT ATTICA SAYS PAROLE BOARD SHOULD SET TERMS

CANTON, N. Y. (AP) — The warden of Attica Prison says the State Parole Board, rather than judges, should determine how much time a prisoner spends behind bars.

Warden Walter B. Martin told the 10th annual Moran Institute on Delinquency and Crime Thursday night that prisoners would behave better and would be easier to rehabilitate under his proposal.

The institute is sponsored jointly by St. Lawrence University and state agencies that deal with criminals. The six-day meeting ends today.

He noted that persons confined to state hospitals for the insane were released when hospital officials felt they were ready to return to society. Martin suggested a similar system for prisons. The parole board would make the decisions.

Under present law, a prisoner is not eligible for parole until he has served a specific portion of a sentence imposed by a judge.

STEEL UNION HEAD ASKS FEDERAL HELP

Statement Seen as Hope Of Government Intervention in Strike

NEW YORK (AP)—The head of the steel union has indicated it would welcome increased federal participation in efforts to settle the nationwide steel industry strike.

David J. McDonald, president of the United Steelworkers of America, says: "In view of the size

FINALLY IN CUSTODY—Theodore Holton sits glumly between two troopers at Troop A Barracks this morning after being captured under the front steps of the Community Building at the Tonawanda Indian Reservation. Sgt. William A. Rimmer, left, and Trooper K. E. Limner show sawed-off .22 caliber rifle found next to Holton at the time of his capture.

FALLOUT SHELTERS COMMITTEE NAMED

Governor Going Ahead With Controversial Plan for Legislature

ALBANY, N. Y. (AP) — Gov. Rockefeller is forging ahead with a controversial plan to have fall

Leading Police Wild Chase Gave Elusive Holton "Kick"

Smiling for the first time since his capture near the Tonawanda Indian Reservation this morning, Teddy Holton replied "sure" when asked by a newsman if he got a "kick" out of eluding police.

Handcuffed and guarded by two troopers at the Troop A Barracks on East Main St., Holton mumbled: "I like to sit back and watch them

shooting at his pursuers on other occasions, Holton replied:

"I wouldn't shoot at them. Maybe into the air to scare them a little. I fired three shots in the air when Johns saw me just to shake him up a little." The shots, he admitted, came from a .22 caliber rifle.

"I pinned a note on Bock's (Un-

But it only took one "Teddy" Holton to turn Indian Falls upside down.

Holton, 20, a three-time escapee from Rochester State Hospital—this time two days ago, out a bathroom window and down the drainpipe—is of little concern to Indian Falls residents on July 14, 1959. But a few days later, when he emerges from the brush between the Tonawanda Reservation and Route 77 and fires three shots at Deputy Sheriff Merton Johns with a .22 caliber rifle, he has their full attention—for the rifle was taken from the home of neighbor Johnny Adams, a Genesee County deputy, while Adams was away on a fishing trip.

Holton leads the police on several wild-goose chases, each time disappearing and then reappearing some distance away. Once, after failing to capture the elusive will-o'-the-wisp, Deputy Sheriff Sam Bock returns to his patrol car and finds a handwritten note, "Ha, Ha, you missed me."

On July 23, the will-o'-the-wisp is still on the lam.

"It is possible he could have gone all the way to Orleans County in the woods," a reporter said. "The only times he would need to leave the wooded areas would be for dashes across roads and across Tonawanda Creek."

Now 75 law enforcement officers, armed with rifles, shotguns, and submachine guns, as well as a bloodhound, search in vain. Even the bloodhound's trained nose fails its task. The searchers, plagued by mosquitoes, wonder how Holton can stand it.

Then, a tip from Laverne Kruger, who works the Etzold farm several miles away in Corfu—he just encountered Holton in the milkhouse, and Holton is running through a beanfield toward Etzold's barn.

When the searchers reach the barn, Holton is already in the hay mow. He leaps out a side window, dropping 25 feet to the ground, and disappears into a cornfield.

Unaware he has escaped, the troopers and deputies strip to the waist and move all the bales of hay out of the mow; the temperature up there is well over 100 degrees. Now Holton is wanted in four counties, for car theft (joyrides) and break-ins. Finally, on July 31, he is dragged from his hiding place under the steps of the Tonawanda Reservation's community house, feet first.

What the police didn't know was that Holton had an accomplice—Rosie Emerson—who lived up the road from Boulder Park. She was transporting him from place to place.

"Those who didn't know Teddy were scared, but those who did were all laughing," chuckles Lois Brockway, Town of Pembroke historian. "He was playing games with the cops."

In the early 1960s, to keep attendance high, Phil strikes a deal with Sam Herrington, a New York Central signalman and railroad hobbyist. Sam and three partners, all railroad men, have designed and built a 14-gauge steam railroad. They bring the ride to Boulder Park, where it circles a mile-long track through the woods on the opposite side of the creek.

Now visitors cross the footbridge in both directions—

Above: Sam Herrington's miniature steam train crosses a trestle at its new location, its second. Author's collection.

Below: Herrington's train in its first location, at Boulder Park. The train was an immensely popular ride. Courtesy Town of Pembroke historian.

Francis Gailee rides the deer on Emilie's carrousel.

The new train bought to replace Sam Herrington's steam train. It operated on the south side of the creek, on the land between the creek and Indian Falls Road. Phil Morrot is operating the train. The footbridge over the creek is in the background. Courtesy the Morrot family.

to and from the new "Boulder Park Railroad," with its shrill whistle, chugging sounds, and genuine smoke and cinders.

One day Phil notices tickets are being resold and hires a spotter to catch the dishonesty in the act. Then he and Sam exchange bitter words, and Phil orders Sam to leave. Phil replaces Sam's train with a new, modern train (built by a friend of Walt Disney, who used the same hydraulic brake system on Disney's monorail system in California).

Sam retaliates by putting his steam train directly across the road from where it was, directly competing for Phil's business. Phil, in turn, erects a high fence along Indian Falls Road to contain his customers. The neighbors and people driving by are displeased by it all; the barricade is an eyesore.

The bitter feud continues, and Phil is served with a notice to remove the fence. He refuses and is backed by a restraining order protecting his property. Ultimately, the New York State Supreme Court settles the matter, and the fence comes down.

It is July 1963, Phil is 73, and he has achieved what he set out to accomplish. He decides to retire; this will be his last season.

But before that happens, he grabs the upper hand once more—but only after he gets blood poisoning in it (from cleaning the merry-go-round machinery). When the decision is made to amputate Phil's arm, he refuses to allow it, saying he came into the world with two arms, and he will go out the same way. The doctors manage to save his arm.

As he relates this, Paul is reminded of other examples of his father's tenacity—including Phil's victory over the broken-skull bogey.

"How that happened, my dad had a small Gibson tractor, as few tractors were available after World War II," he explains. "It had a Wisconsin engine up front and no hood. You'd steer with a lever that moved back and forth, instead of a steering wheel. It had power, and it worked great for cleaning the park—you could jump off and on, and it was easy to steer.

"Father was riding on the tow bar that day. He jumped off and told me to head back to the park, that he'd walk.

"Just as I started out, he changed his mind and jumped back on. When he did, he hit my arm and shoulder, which sent the lever forward and the tractor to the left. It threw him onto the right rear wheel and up into the air. He came

Lucille and King. Lucille occasionally envied children who came to the park to play and didn't have to work. But she says, "I had a wonderful childhood. So many good memories." King was a popular performer; he danced for hot dogs, which boosted hot dog sales at the park. Courtesy the Morrot family.

down on his head, on the pavement, fracturing his skull.

"Johnny Adams and I loaded him in the back seat of his 1942 Olds-mobile, and we drove to the doctor in the big white house in Corfu—but the doctor wasn't there. The nurse told us, take him directly to the emergency room and keep him upright with his head tilted back, because he is unconscious and having difficulty breathing.

"We took off for Batavia, and I mean Adams was running wide open. When we got there, there was a line of traffic, so he drove on the sidewalk, passing traffic on the right. He stayed on the sidewalk all the way to St. Jerome Hospital.

"Mrs. Adams took Lucille home with her to keep her from telling my mother, and wouldn't let her go home until they heard something.

"We didn't think Father was gonna make it. He was bleeding from the ears, too.

"But he did."

Although Phil's tenacity is remarkable, it is his generosity the community still remembers. For example, he would contribute graciously whenever asked for a donation, and he welcomed disabled children to Boulder Park, providing free-admission days especially for them.

Front: Lucille rides the carousel in 1955. The person in front is Phyllis Wade. Courtesy the Morrot family.

Ramblin' Lou, a popular country-western singer, along with Zeke Corey, continued to draw crowds at Boulder Park for many years. Company picnics also drew large crowds, such as those put on by Dunlop tire and Rubber Co., Certainteed, and National Gypsum. Courtesy the Morrot family.

"It was amazing, some of the kids who came there, who only had one foot or something. They still played the games, and they really enjoyed the park," Paul says.

"He'd contact the hospitals and the school for the blind in Batavia, and he'd tell them, if you ever want to bring the kids, they're welcome—and they'd bring them in. The park opened at 1 p.m., but if the kids arrived at 9 or 10 in the morning, it was understood that we opened for them.

"When the Indian Falls Methodists had men's suppers at the church, my mother would fix something, and my father and I would go. Sometimes we showed comedy films, to create good rapport," Paul relates.

"My dad did everything he could to gain the community's acceptance. We had two strikes against us, however—we were Catholics in a Methodist community, and we were considered "carny" people. But we weren't carnies—we were in the outdoor amusement business, a park situation. You can't compare the two, as far as operations are concerned."

Although the Morrots didn't realize it then, the community respected and appreciated the family for its high standards and dedication to family-oriented entertainment at a low price.

Boulder Park, in fact, was called "the best deal going."

Phil kept prices low by doing much of the work himself and by constructing many of his own games. He made the familiar cast-aluminum milk bottles, for example, at the foundry in Lockport.

"We'd set up either five or ten of the bottles, and the people would throw balls to try to knock them down. If we had a wide enough area, we'd have three setups. They'd get three balls for a dime," Paul explains.

"The balls were made of string, which is how baseballs were made then, and the leather was gone off of them. The carnies weighted their bottles, so they'd rock back and forth but not fall down. But my father didn't."

And, convinced of its value, he didn't skimp on the band organ music. He kept the tunes current.

"Every year when we went to get new music, we'd take a list of songs my mother had made—her favorites were "Over the Waves," "Beer Barrel Polka," "I'm Looking Over a Four-Leaf Clover," "Sentimental Journey," and "Faraway Places." We'd drop the band organ off for service in the fall and pick it up in the spring, along with a new music roll. The rolls were custom selections for $25. Ralph Tussig would play the songs while the machine punched the paper rolls."

He describes how his father repainted the rides and the carousel figures every year, to keep them looking new, and the method he used for striping. "He striped everything," Paul laughs. "He used this special contraption—a small glass bottle with an adapter, a built-in guide, and different-sized wheels. He would use one wheel for a thin stripe or a couple together for wider stripes."

Paul contemplates the contraption he is holding. "The last stripe my father painted was yellow," he says.

Phil officially retired and sold Boulder Park on May 15, 1964, in time for the new owner, Wilbert Stradtman, to open that season.

One of Phil's last days at Boulder Park—in the main ticket booth. He sold the park on May 15, 1964, to Wilbert Stradtman.

Boulder Park's new owner, Wilbert Stradtman, in 1964. Courtesy the Morrot family.

The apple dryer and merry-go-round buildings are still
standing in this photograph of the Boulder Park site in
1992. Photograph by Cyndy Hanks.

QUIETUS

Late summer 1992, Indian Falls. Today is a lazy, kick-back-and-smell-the-flowers day: even Mother Nature is in slow gear. Little has changed since 1970, yet everything has changed. The silence is unfamiliar, more like a hush; the hamlet is once again frozen in time, suspended in a state of expectation.

Something happened here—you can feel it. In clusters, people talk reverently of a magical time when everything, even the flowers, bloomed brighter. Yet they appear content, as they were before they were charmed—but caught in the moments before a surprise. In their daydreams, the silence will shatter, the day will turn upside down, and their televisions will be forgotten as they ride the magic horses. Actually, they will laugh, amuse themselves, and rejoice with the dragonflies, butterflies, and fireflies, who teach us that life is never quite what it appears, but always is filled with color and light.

Occasionally a katydid sings, its imperious song trailing off into the silence. A cricket joins in and then a tree toad. Now the lazy, liquid lapping of a flowing creek, leaves rustling in the topmost branches of the hickory trees, distant laughter from a family gathering, an occasional chirp as a songbird flits by—gone are the faintly remembered sounds of yesterday, of an amusement park in its heyday.

They are all gone, too—all of the people. Now the only visitors to the site are water snakes and four-footed creatures—raccoons, possum, skunks, skinks, and woodchucks. Occasionally lovers and vagrants will tramp through, but generally the weeds discourage them.

To the bogey, it is paradise.

Claire and Phil Morrot. Phil dies in an automobile accident on July 23, 1968 at 77. Claire dies of a brain tumor on March 24, 1970.

All that was left of the popular footbridge that crossed to the other side of Tonawanda Creek. Photo by Cyndy Hanks, 1992.

Emilie's carrousel at International Village, outside Gettysburg, Pennsylvania. Photographs taken in 1977, courtesy of Charles J. Jacques, Jr., © Charles J. Jacques, Jr.

The wait was worthwhile—and waiting was required, for the young man was amazingly determined and resilient. But ultimately, the bogey has achieved its objectives: It has silenced the chatter, claimed the prize property, and dismantled and scattered the silly carrousel.

It didn't all happen at once, or entirely as planned, but none of that matters now.. What does matter is, the job is done.

Phil Morrot died July 25, 1968, in an automobile accident within two miles of his retirement home in Florida. He was driving Paul's second car at the time—a 1957 Chevy—on his way to pick up his own car from a body shop. The other car ran a stop sign.

Claire Morrot, in her second year of widowhood, died March 24, 1970, of a brain tumor.

Boulder Park closed, never to reopen, after the 1970 season.

Wilbert Stradtman, under whose ownership Boulder Park declined, died in February 1972.

Paul Morrot and Lucille Morrot Walters, despite a last-ditch effort to save Boulder Park by reclaiming it, reluctantly sold it in July 1973. They simply could not afford to operate it from a distance.

The new owner sold the rides the following year, including the carrousel.

Emilie's carrousel resurfaced in 1977 at International Village, an amusement area at a Sheraton hotel and convention center south of Gettysburg, Pennsylvania. International Village—a failed pipe dream—lasted only a year.

THE AUCTION
NEW YORK CITY   DECEMBER 16, 1989

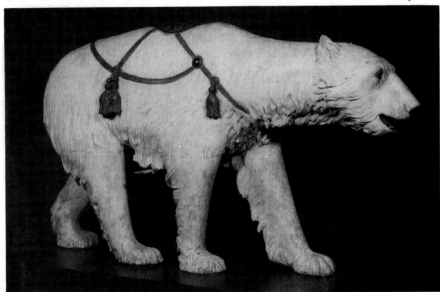

The Allan Herschell Polar Bear. The singular landmark piece that brought to the attention of serious collectors of fine American carvings the significance of the carousel figure. Just one of the 180 vintage figures included in the premiere auction in the carousel field to be conducted in New York's Pier 88 on December 16.

To learn more about morning. The exact schedule appears in the comprehensive catalogue ($28 by mail available from Guernsey's) which will also include an exceptional selection of Cigar Store Indians (including the very fine Punchinello pictured) and other interesting American wood carvings to be sold during this auction.

WORLD RECORD AUCTION PRICES

A SUMMARY OF THE HIGHEST PRICES PAID AT
PUBLICALLY ADVERTISED AUCTIONS
WHERE EVERYONE WAS GIVEN EQUAL OPPORTUNITY TO BID.

Updated January, 1990
(Previous list in July, 1989 issue)

Buyer's premiums are included in the prices listed where applicable, as that was the total price paid to own the item. Sales tax is not included.

TOP SELLING MENAGERIE ANIMALS

1.	2-89	Dentzel Rooster	Sotheby's	$148,500
2.	12-89	Allan Herschell Polar Bear	Guernsey's	121,000
3.	4-89	Dentzel Mascot Lion ..... Coney Island Mus.	Guernsey's	110,000
4.	12-88	Dentzel Tiger	Guernsey's	83,600
5.	12-88	Allan Hersch. Elephant . Waldameer	Guernsey's	72,600
6.	12-89	Dentzel Tiger .... Great Escape	Guernsey's	63,800
7.	10-89	E. Joy Morris Lion ...... Quassy	Norton	60,000
8.	5-87	Looff Greyhound	Phillips	59,400
9.	12-89	Dentzel Lion .... Great Escape	Guernsey's	57,200
10.	12-89	Looff Lion .... Eldridge Park	Guernsey's	56,100

Above: The midway buildings. The most popular were the Skeeball, fish pond, ring toss, and bottle games, and the cotton candy and popcorn stand.

Below: The familiar "welcome" sign at the entrance to Boulder Park. There was a much larger, lighted sign there, as well.

Below, right: The millrace near the creek, after the water was diverted. Photographs by Cyndy Hanks, 1992.

Ultimately, Edwin Farren III, a New Jersey attorney, accepted the carousel—some have said in lieu of legal fees. Farren stored the figures until October 1983, when he sent his collection to Guernsey's "American Carvings" auction.

The figures stood, covered and unrecognized, awaiting their fate. The Allan Herschell polar bear, a singular piece, created a stir. Until then, collectors of carousel art had not seen such a figure. New York folk-art collectors Joel and Kate Kopp paid a then-record price of $28,600 (including buyer's premium) for the bear; they sold it the following January for $48,000.

The lion, tiger, camel, giraffe, elephant, deer, and plumed charger all went their separate ways. In December 1989, the polar bear reappeared on the block, this time a celebrity. At this auction, the bear brought $121,000.

"The Allan Herschell Polar Bear and the Illions High Mane were the 'best of the best,'" wrote Rusty Donahue, of Americana Antiques, in *Carousel News & Trader*. "The Allan Herschell polar bear sold for $26,000 at the Ferren sale, and within six years it sold again for $121,000." It was the world's second highest price ever paid at auction for a menagerie carousel figure.

As time went on, more unusual figures appeared in carousel books and magazines, all of them from Emilie's carrousel—all incorrectly identified and without any reference to Emilie's ride. The carousel world wondered about each, What is its true history?

Now, today, an intruder, having gotten permission and struggling through the thick undergrowth and trees with a camera, is on

the old midway, poking about the derelict buildings. She is taking photographs. The merry-go-round building is open, and she enters.

She snaps the familiar sign with its promise of "Fun Fun Fun." She moves the ice cream sign closer to a window and captures it in the light. Snap. Vintage soft drink machines. Snap.

Old tickets. Snap.

Three weeks later, she is back, with permission to remove objects and return them to the Morrot family—but now the merry-to-round building is completely empty. An old car sits inside, with the hood up. Someone has been working on it.

"The oil paintings from the ride should be there," Paul had explained, "rolled up against one of the back walls, behind some stuff. You won't realize what they are until you unroll them." But nothing is there—the building has been cleaned out.

A disheveled young man stokes a smoldering pile of rubble nearby. "What happened?" she asked, stunned. "Where is everything?"

The young man smiles a lazy, country smile, the smile of a bogey. "I had myself a great fire today," he replies.

"Those old wood signs, tickets, all that junk—*POOF!*— you should have seen it go!"

Above: The hand-lettered ice cream sign and popular refreshment stand, which was built "like a cabinet."

Below: The merry-go-round building.

Below, left: Some items in the building before everything left inside was burned. Photographs by Cyndy Hanks, 1992.

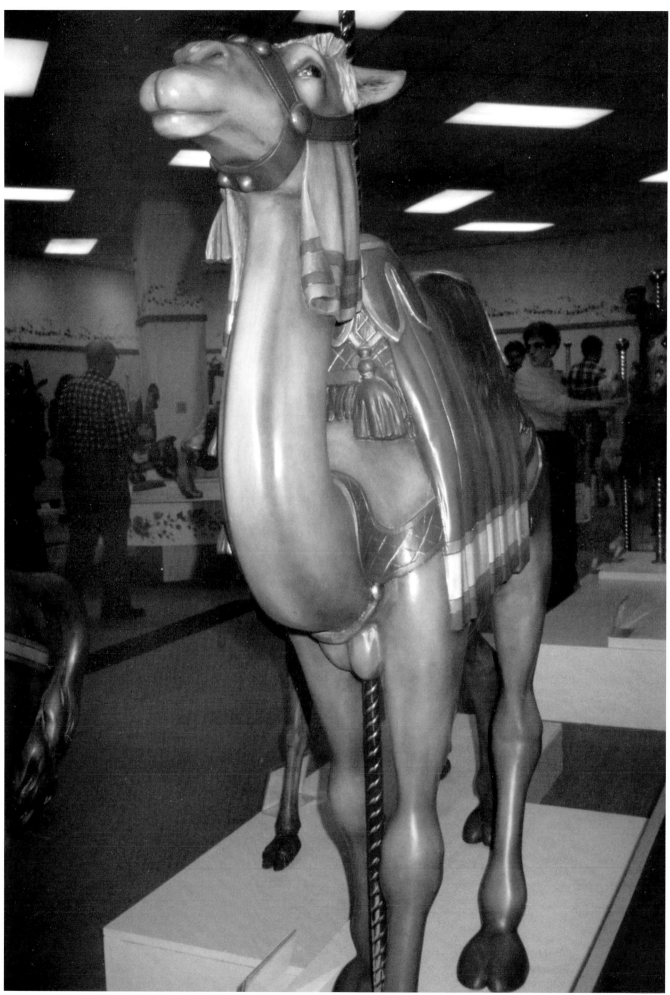

102 *The camel on exhibit in St. Louis, from the American Carousel Museum, supported by the Freels Foundation. Photograph by Cyndy Hanks, 1992.*

EPILOGUE

The polar bear was the first to reveal itself, loping side-ways across a right-hand page in *Americana*. It appeared to be moving purposefully toward yet another new home at the time of publication, after attracting an incredibly high price at a Guernsey's New York City auction iin December 1989.

Since it appeared to have traveled alone without any mention of other related figures, the first question—What happened to Emilie's carrousel?—had a definite answer. Obviously, the ride had been broken up, and its menagerie figures had gone their separate ways.

Several calls to determine who currently owned the polar bear in 1992 brought the expected response and the first of many dead ends—"The bear's current owner wishes to remain anonymous."

The owner did respond graciously to a forwarded letter, however, which included a factory photo of his treasure and identifying information. On the condition of anonymity, would he talk? Even better, would he agree to a visit? He did, and the bear was joyously pho-tographed from every angle. A year or two later, the owner agreed to a second visit, for the purpose of reuniting Lucille Morrot with the big white companion of her childhood.

Theirs was a tearful reunion, and the bear—which had been carefully restored to its original factory paint— was hugged several times. It has since been sold again; the current owner also wishes to remain anonymous.

The second figure to reveal itself was the original, oversized elephant, but the search was complicated by at least four slightly smaller look-alikes made by the Allan Herschell factory after it completed the first.

The side view of the Allan Herschell polar bear has become a familiar image, but few have experienced its endearing smile. Despite the number of times the image has been reproduced, where it came from has remained a mystery. Courtesy the owner, who has requested anonymity. Photograph by Cyndy Hanks, 1992.

Above: The original elephant, restored and elaborately redecorated. Lucille remembers seeing the elephant in a museum, with a plaque that correctly identified it. The owner, Earl Corey, of Ohio, purchased this elephant from a museum, but by then the plaque was missing. The elephant matches the factory photograph exactly, except for the placement of two tassels— they appear to have been replaced. Photograph courtesy Earl Corey.

Left: Lucille and Earl Corey, confirming the identity of the elephant. Photograph by Cyndy Hanks, 1992.

Once when I visited Lucille, she discovered a piece of paper bearing the word "elephant" and a phone number. Lacking any other clues, we placed the call, and Earl Corey answered; he said he had a large Allan Herschell elephant in his collection. He invited us to bring the factory photographs, for comparison. Earl's elephant was definitely larger than the look-alikes, and it appeared identical to the factory photograph except for the positioning of two tassels—they appeared to have been replaced. We concluded Earl's elephant was the too-large elephant on Emilie's ride.

The replacement elephant was purchased by the late Charlotte Dinger and is part of her collection at Carousel World Museum at Peddlers Village in Lahaska, Pennsylvania.

The camel came to *us*—twice. The first time, Lucille and I paused to admire a camel at the Merry-Go-Round Museum in Sandusky, Ohio. We did not realize the camel was Emilie's. After we compared it with the factory photograph, however, it was easy to confirm its identity. A year or so later, when the

Above: Emilie's camel (back) at Sandusky's Merry-Go-Round Museum, on loan from the American Carousel Museum. Lucille Morrot and the author paused to admire the camels duriing a visit there. Lucille said, "That camel in back looks like ours." A comparison with the camel in the factory photograph prompted the comment, "That was our camel!" The other two were carved by Charles I. D. Looff. Photograph courtesy American Carousel Museum, supported by the Freels Foundation.

Below: The polar bear has moved again since this photograph was taken. Photograph by Cyndy Hanks, 1992.

Above: The "romance" side of a carousel horse is the most ornate. Emilie's armored lead horse bears a Crusader's shield.

Below: The inner side of the horse is plainer. Photographs courtesy Lourinda Bray.

National Carousel Association convened in St. Louis, the camel appeared again, on exhibit.

Lourinda Bray, owner of Running Horse Studio in Pasadena, purchased Emilie's black charger, the fancy armored lead horse with the plume, at Guernsey's 1983 auction. The horse was painted just as it looks on page 100 of *Art of the Carousel*, by Charlotte Dinger.

She stripped it clean, repaired minor seam separations and an ear tip, and sharpened a few worn edges. Because the horse was in fairly good condition, the entire restoration process took only 11 days, "which is very good time," Lourinda explains.

She describes many differences between Emilie's armored horse and the typical Allan Herschell horses.

"The body of this horse has a heavier appearance and a more bullet-shaped rear," she explains. "The croup is a bit lower—it would be called 'goose-rumped' on a live horse. The body is six inches longer and 1.5 to 2 inches wider than the usual Allan Herschell outside-row horses.

"The leg positions are those of a second-row jumper, not a first-row jumper—meaning the left front leg is raised instead of the right, and the rear legs are drawn forward but drop lower in the rear.

"The feathering on the legs is much more pronounced than on later outer-row horses (earlier legs were smooth with just a few veins or grooves to indicate hair at the back of the ankle). The armored horse's feathering goes more than halfway up the lower leg, but the foot hairs do not go onto the hooves. The neck is a bit longer, probably because of the bigger, longer body.

"The tongue is big, with a large mound at the back, and the teeth are very long—as if they should have gums carved into them.

"The mane hangs down in loose, undefined waves, instead of having hanks of hair pulled forward. The tail is fuller and has a smoother profile than the bulged top of the usual Allan Herschell horse—and there are more sections of hair carved into it. The head tucks back more toward the shoulder.

"The saddle is flat at the cantle, with the same pommel, and the bear's head hangs lower over the hip toward the leg. On other Allan Herschells, the bear's head is *on* the hip, and its eyes are always open, looking at you. This bear's eyes are closed."

Restoring Emilie's charger was easy for Lourinda. "My hand naturally strokes out Allan Herschell and Herschell-Spillman patterns," she says.

An interior designer purchased the lion at Guernsey's 1983 auction, and it appeared in a national design magazine in the mid-1980s, but its whereabouts now is unknown. The giraffe (minus

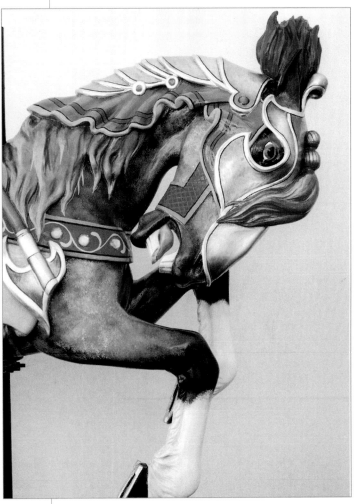

The lead horse is typically the most magnificent horse on the ride and faces out when the ride comes to a stop. Emilie's black charger was just fully restored in more pleasing colors by Lourinda Bray's Running Horse Studio in Pasadena. Photograph courtesy of Lourinda Bray.

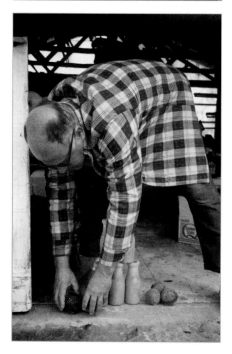

its ears) was also purchased at the 1983 auction, and its whereabouts, too, is unknown.

But Phil's and Emilie's dreams live on.

In September 2001, more than 30 years after its demise, Boulder Park was ceremonially honored; an official marker was placed at the former park site to recognize its historic significance.

And slowly—one astonishing figure at a time—Emilie's carrousel is reappearing; we believe we have just identified another horse.

Left, top: Paul and Lucille Morrot. Paul is retired from the Leesburg, Florida, police force. He and his family live in Florida. Lucille and her family live in Ohio (1992).

Left, middle: Edna Greenhagle (front) and some of her neighbors at the annual "Brick House Corners Fair," which is held near Indian Falls in the town of Pembroke. Edna and her family lived in the one-room schoolhouse at Indian Falls for many years after they converted it to a house (2001).

Left, bottom: Paul Morrot demonstrates the bottle game. His father made the cast-aluminum milk bottles at the foundry in Lockport, New York (1992).

Above: Lucille Morrot and the author the day the historic marker was placed at the former Boulder Park site to recognize the significance of Emilie's carrousel and the achievement of Phil's dream (2001). Photographs by Cyndy Hanks.

ACKNOWLEDGMENTS

Cover Design - Sandy Knight
Book Design - Cyndy Hennig Hanks
Editorial Support - Ceil Goldman
Printing - EPI Printing & Finishing, Inc.

And thanks to the following:
Lois Brockway, Town of Pembroke historian
Pembroke Historical Society
Lucille Morrot Walters, daughter of Theophilus Morrot
Paul Morrot, son of Theophilus Morrot
Rose Babb, granddaughter of Eugene Morrot
Charles Matteson
Brian Morgan, president, National Carousel Association
Marianne Stevens, president, American Carousel Society
Brian Steptoe, fairground and carnival author, England
Lourinda Bray, Running Horse Studio
Elizabeth Brick, Herschell Carrousel Factory Museum
Frank Starr, Corning Museum of Glass
Corning Museum of Glass Research Library
Jane Voelpl and Rosemary Sansone, Olcott Beach Carousel Park
Niagara County Historical Society
Reference staff, Lockport Public Library
John L. Eckerson, Town of Newstead
Judson H. Heck, Town of Newfane historian
Rosemary Promenschenkel, Streatorland Historical Society
Joan M. Oliver, Salem Community College Library
Ellie Kidd, archives manager, Salem County Clerk
Salem County Historical Society
Francis Hanks, my husband, for his support

Amalie, Rose, and Eugene Morrot. Rose was born on January 31, 1919, in Petersburg, Virginia, many years after her brother and sister. Pete (August 5, 1902) and Jennie (March 24, 1906) were born in France. Rose is Rose Babb's mother. Courtesy Rose Babb.

ABOUT THE AUTHOR

Cyndy Hennig Hanks, APR, grew up in Indian Falls, where she rode the Boulder Park carrousel as a child. She has been a professional writer and consultant for nearly 20 years and editor of the National Carousel Association's *Merry-Go-Roundup* magazine for more than a decade.

She is a member of the George Eastman House Council, Go Art!, the Herschell Carrousel Factory Museum, the National Amusement Park Historical Association, the Public Relations Society of America (PRSA), the Strong Museum, and Women in Communications.

In 1995, Hanks received a PRism award for *Merry-Go-Roundup* from PRSA and was named to PRSA's Counselor's Academy in 1996. She served as vice president and director of public relations for two national advertising agencies based in Rochester, New York, over a span of 11 years.

She lives in Penfield, New York, with her husband, the Rev. Francis Hanks, and is actively involved in the children's ministry at Rochester Baptist Church.